M000283771

They echoed the voice of God

Reflections on the Minor Prophets

Roger Ellsworth

DayOne

© Day One Publications 2008
First Edition 2008

Unless otherwise indicated, Scripture quotations are from the New King
James Version (NKJV)®. Copyright © 1982 by Thomas Nelson, Inc. Used by
permission. All rights reserved.

British Library Cataloguing in Publication Data available

ISBN 978-1-84625-101-6

Published by Day One Publications
Ryelands Road, Leominster, HR6 8NZ

☎ 01568 613 740
FAX: 01568 611 473
email—sales@dayone.co.uk
web site—www.dayone.co.uk

Designed by Wayne McMaster and printed by Gutenberg Press, Malta

Dedicated to my good friends,
Larry and Terry Toms

Commendations

In this excellent book on the Minor Prophets, Roger Ellsworth gives the reader a clear understanding of the importance of these neglected and often underestimated books of the Bible. As the author says in his introduction, 'These were men with a big God.' Setting each prophet in his times, Roger Ellsworth goes on to show clearly how all of these men demonstrated the greatness of God in their message—a message as essential for our day as it was for theirs. Laced with helpful, practical application, this book shows how each prophet emphasized a particular aspect of God's character, giving an overall picture that is compelling.

Jim Winter, Minister of Horsell Evangelical Church, Woking, England

Biblical prophets were spokesmen for God. Through them the Lord revealed his word, his will and, most notably, himself. Roger Ellsworth helps us appreciate how the so-called Minor Prophets make known the character and work of our great God. This book is a great introduction to and overview of their prophecies. Read it to become acquainted with these sometimes overlooked servants and, more importantly, with the unchangeable God whose message they proclaimed.

Tom Ascol, Director of Founders Ministries and Pastor, Grace Baptist Church, Cape Coral, Florida, USA

Acknowledgements

As always, I appreciate the assistance of my dear wife, Sylvia, in the preparation of these pages. My sincere thanks also go to the congregation of Immanuel Baptist Church for gladly joining me in this tour of the Minor Prophets.

Contents

Introduction

How big is your Bible? Does it contain sixty-six books? Or are some missing? Many people are carrying Bibles with missing books. The books are actually there, but they are virtually non-existent because they are never used.

Here is another question: How big is your God?

It is sadly possible to carry a little Bible and believe in a little God.

In the following chapters, we will be examining one passage from each of the twelve Minor Prophets.

Getting acquainted with these men will certainly make our Bibles bigger. No books of the Bible are more neglected than these! By the way, let's get this nailed down: the Minor Prophets are 'minor' only because of the size of their books. We must never think they are minor in significance.

As we study these prophecies, we shall soon discover that these were men with a big God. They made sense of their circumstances and found strength for their challenges by basking in a sense of the God who was above it all and in it all. The God they served was wise enough to plan and strong enough to achieve. He was the purposeful God who was ordering all circumstances according to his will. He was the just God who refused to ignore sin, but he was also the God of all grace. No sin was too great for him to pardon. No force could ever make him let go of his people and his purpose.

We need the message of the Minor Prophets because we are definitely living in the days of the 'little God'. The 'little

God' is the one whose worship is far from majestic, resembling instead a carnival atmosphere. He is one whose truth does not weigh heavily on his people. He is one who does not inspire his people to obey his commandments and does not thrill them with his promises. The 'little God' is much more concerned about getting his people comfortably through another week than he is about getting them safely into eternity.

There are plenty of things to lament in the professing church these days, but she has no deficiency that cannot be cured by a larger vision of her God.

If our great and good God chooses to use these chapters to instil in some that larger vision, I will count myself very happy indeed.

The Prophet
Hosea

Our welcoming God

O Israel, *return to the* LORD *your God, for you have stumbled because of your iniquity;*

Take words with you, and return to the LORD. *Say to Him, 'Take away all iniquity; receive us graciously, for we will offer the sacrifices of our lips.*

Assyria shall not save us, we will not ride on horses, nor will we say anymore to the work of our hands, "You are our gods." For in You the fatherless finds mercy.'

'I will heal their backsliding, I will love them freely, for My anger has turned away from him. I will be like the dew to Israel; he shall grow like the lily, and lengthen his roots like Lebanon.

His branches shall spread; his beauty shall be like an olive tree, and his fragrance like Lebanon.

Those who dwell under his shadow shall return; they shall be revived like grain, and grow like a vine. Their scent shall be like the wine of Lebanon. Ephraim shall say, "What have I to do anymore with idols?" I have heard and observed him. I am like a green cypress tree; your fruit is found in Me.'

Who is wise? Let him understand these things. Who is prudent? Let him know them. For the ways of the LORD *are right; the righteous walk in them, but transgressors stumble in them.*

Hosea 14:1–9

Hosea ministered to the nation of Israel from 754 to 714 BC. Most of his ministry took place before the nation was carried into captivity by the Assyrians in 722 BC.

Hosea's was a dreadful, awful time. From the time it split

from the house of David, the kingdom of Israel went headlong into idolatrous worship (1 Kings 12:1–33).

There were other grievous things going on as well, as the Lord so plainly declared:

> There is no truth or mercy
> Or knowledge of God in the land.
> By swearing and lying,
> Killing and stealing and committing adultery,
> They break all restraint,
> With bloodshed upon bloodshed.
>
> (Hosea 4:1b–2)

There has never been a more unusual prophet than Hosea. He was called by God to marry an immoral woman who would prove to be unfaithful to him. God intended to make Hosea's marriage a picture of the whole nation of Israel. Just as Hosea was married to Gomer, so God was married to Israel; and just as Gomer was unfaithful to Hosea, so Israel was unfaithful to God.

Do we find Hosea already speaking to us? The truth is that every Christian is in a marital relationship with God, and every Christian is called, therefore, to be faithful to God. When we give to anything else the love and devotion that belong to God alone, we are guilty of unfaithfulness. We are guilty of spiritual adultery!

What does your heart tell you, believer, about your relationship to the Lord? Have you been faithful? Are you giving the Lord the love that you should? Are you giving him your time? Are you faithful to his house?

Now here is the wonderful, encouraging message from the 'nugget' I have chosen from this little prophecy: we can come back to God because he is our welcoming God!

Our welcoming God tells us why we need to return (v. 1)

Throughout his prophecy, Hosea has sounded the terrible notes of sin and judgement, but in this last chapter, he sounds the joyful note of hope. His message of hope is built around the word 'return', a word which he uses fifteen times in this prophecy.

This word conveys a most glorious truth indeed. We can come back to God! No matter how far we stray and how miserably we fail, we can come back to God! Could there be a more blessed truth? The people of Israel had turned their backs on God and had turned their faces towards sin. They had spurned God and embraced sin. The Lord here calls them to reverse what they had previously done. He calls them to turn their backs on their sins and turn their faces towards him.

The people of Israel needed to return to God because they had 'stumbled' because of their 'iniquity'.

Sin always makes us stumble. We cannot walk uprightly before God and walk in sin. We cannot walk close to God and walk in sin.

The New International Version translates the clause 'you have stumbled because of your iniquity' in this way: 'Your sins have been your downfall!'

The devil would have us believe that sin is the way to happiness, satisfaction and fulfilment. The truth is just the opposite. Sin is the way to heartache, misery and ruin. Cain, Lot, Esau, Saul and Judas Iscariot are some examples of men who painfully learned the truth about sin.

Our welcoming God tells us how to return (vv. 2–3)

Hosea was not content simply to urge the people to return to God. He also told them how to do this. They were to 'take words' with them as they came back to God. There was to be a real conversation with God.

This is what the prodigal son did when he returned to his father (Luke 15:21). This is what David did when he returned to the Lord after sinning so grievously (Ps. 51).

The apostle John writes, 'If we confess our sins, He is faithful and just to forgive us our sins and to cleanse us from all unrighteousness' (1 John 1:9).

It is not enough, of course, merely to mouth empty words without sincerity of heart. Those words must come from hearts that are broken with the enormity of the sin. They must be words which ask God to take away the iniquity and graciously to forgive. They must include words of renunciation. Just as the nation of Israel was to renounce an alliance with Assyria as the means for achieving future security (v. 3), so our own return to God must feature a true renunciation of our dependence on every other resource as well as of our idols.

Our welcoming God promises to receive and restore us when we return (vv. 4–8)

These are some of the most heart-warming verses in the Bible. The Lord here pictures his willingness to receive and restore his wayward people.

It is so hard for us to believe that God is truly willing to forgive us. We believe it for a while, and then the devil comes along and tells us that it cannot be.

We can be assured that it was the same with Hosea's people. Knowing this difficulty, the Lord portrayed his forgiveness in one way and then in another.

PICTURES OF FORGIVENESS (VV. 4–5)

Healing (v. 4)

He tells them that he will 'heal their backsliding'. Here is a man who has suffered long with a terrible disease. He has had surgery and taken various treatments. Then one day his doctor says, 'You may now consider yourself healed.'

What a pleasant word! And that is the word God uses here. Backsliding is a terrible disease for which God offers complete healing.

Loving freely (v. 4)

He also tells them that he will 'love them freely'. We all know what it is to have people be cool and reserved towards us. God is promising here to love his people warmly and without reserve. God receives backsliders spontaneously and warmly. He never makes returning difficult! Once again, we can look at the parable of the prodigal son for a picture of how God receives backsliders.

Refreshing (v. 5)

God also promises to be 'like the dew to Israel'. Just as the dew brings refreshment to a parched land, so the Lord promises to refresh his people spiritually after their time of spiritual drought.

PICTURES OF THE FORGIVEN (VV. 5–6)

After telling the people what he will do for them, the Lord proceeds to tell them what they will be like. His warm welcome to them will make them 'grow like the lily, and lengthen [their] roots like Lebanon' (v. 5). The Lord also promises that Israel's branches 'shall spread' (v. 6).

When we are backslidden, we are stunted; we are not growing spiritually. But when we return to the Lord, we begin to grow again.

The Lord also promises to make Israel both beautiful and fragrant (v. 6). What does this tell us about the state of being backslidden? That there is an ugliness and unpleasantness about it!

THE EFFECT ON OTHERS (V. 7)

Then the Lord adds a word about the effect Israel's restoration would have on others (v. 7).

Backslidden Christians can exert no beneficial influence on others, but restored ones can.

We can sum it all up by saying that God gives vitality where there is no life, strength where there is weakness, beauty where there is ugliness and usefulness where there is barrenness.

A DIFFERENT ATTITUDE TOWARDS IDOLS (V. 8)

A return to God would cause the people to have a different attitude towards their idols. They would not have any more to do with their false gods but would confess that their fruitfulness would be found only in God. It is impossible to turn to God without turning from idols.

The prophecy of Hosea ends with the Lord making an appeal to his people to understand the issues that are before them (v. 9). If they are wise and discerning, they will recognize the folly of serving idols and will understand that the ways of the Lord are right.

Reflect on these points

1. *Every Christian is in a marital relationship with God, and every Christian is called to be faithful to God. When we give to anything else the love and devotion that belong to God alone, we are guilty of spiritual adultery!*

2. *We can come back to God! No matter how far we stray and how miserably we fail, we can come back to God!*

3. *Sin always makes us stumble. We cannot walk uprightly before God and walk in sin.*

4. *Healing—what a pleasant word! Backsliding is a terrible disease for which God offers complete healing.*

The Prophet
Joel

Our restoring God

'Now, therefore,' says the LORD, 'Turn to Me with all your heart, with fasting, with weeping, and with mourning.'

So rend your heart, and not your garments; return to the LORD your God, for He is gracious and merciful, slow to anger, and of great kindness; and He relents from doing harm.

Who knows if He will turn and relent, and leave a blessing behind Him—a grain offering and a drink offering for the LORD your God?

Blow the trumpet in Zion, consecrate a fast, call a sacred assembly;

Gather the people, sanctify the congregation, assemble the elders, gather the children and nursing babes; let the bridegroom go out from his chamber, and the bride from her dressing room.

Let the priests, who minister to the LORD, weep between the porch and the altar; let them say, 'Spare Your people, O LORD, and do not give Your heritage to reproach, that the nations should rule over them. Why should they say among the peoples, "Where is their God?"'

Then the LORD will be zealous for His land, and pity His people.

Joel 2:12–18

We know very little about Joel. He begins his prophecy by sharing a couple of meagre titbits about himself (his name and his father's name), and then he plunges right into his message.

It was a message that the religious leaders and the people

of Judah urgently needed. And it is a message that we need as well. Yes, it is a very old message (probably delivered around 835 BC), but it has lost none of its punch.

The situation that called for restoration (1:2–4; 2:1–11)

Joel prophesied when his people were standing between two calamities. The first was the army of locusts that had visited the land and ruined the crops (1:2–4). The next was the army of a foreign nation that would invade the land if the people did not repent and turn to God (2:1–11).

God had sent the first army, the locusts, and he was prepared to send the second. But if the people would take to heart the lessons from the first army, they would not have to face the second!

The one thing these calamities had in common was that they were both sent by God as judgement upon the sins of his people.

When we read of God sending calamities upon his people, we are inclined to think ill of him. Joel will not let us do so. As the people stood between these two calamities, Joel gave them a beautiful picture of God. It is the picture of a father who, having disciplined his son, scoops him up in his arms, sets him on his lap and, with tender words, tells him how he, the child, can avoid such discipline in the future.

This is the picture of the restoring God!

The turning that would bring restoration (2:12–18)

What does the Lord say to Judah? What was the way for

them to show that they had learnt their lesson and would not need discipline in the future? It was to turn from their sinful behaviour and to turn to the Lord.

Turn with the heart

'Turn to Me,' says the Lord, 'with all your heart' (see v. 12).

The heart is the Bible's shorthand for the whole person. More particularly, the heart is its shorthand for the mind, the affections and the will.

In urging the people to turn to him with their hearts, the Lord was, then, calling on them to turn their minds to the truth of God, to set their affections on the things of God and deliberately to choose to give priority to God.

A little later, the Lord tells them to rend their hearts and not their garments (v. 13).

It was customary in those days for people to show deep distress by ripping their outer garments. But people got to the place where they would rip their garments to show distress when they didn't really feel it all that much (e.g. Matt. 26:64–65).

So the Lord here tells them that they must not merely feign repentance. John Calvin says, 'Moderate repentance will not do.'[1]

Turn with hope and confidence

They were to repent with the awareness that their repentance mattered.

How can we be confident about this matter of repentance? The Lord gives us the answer:

> Return to the LORD your God,
>
> For He is gracious and merciful,
>
> Slow to anger, and of great kindness;
>
> And He relents from doing harm.
>
> (v. 13)

The next verse tells us that the Lord may very well 'leave a blessing behind Him' (v. 14).

Is it possible that the Lord is drawing a picture for us? The people have stopped following God. It is the duty of every child of God to get behind God and follow him, but we cannot follow sin and follow God. Repentance puts us back where we belong—behind God! When we repent and get behind God, he starts leading us again. We get behind him, and he starts off down the road with us following.

But there is more. When we get behind God again through repentance, we might very well find a blessing such as we had never imagined. The blessing Joel mentioned here was material in nature, as was so often the case under the old covenant. It is more likely, under the new covenant, that it will be spiritual in nature. But it will still be the blessing of God.

Let's learn that sin is ever the robber. It steals our blessings! But repentance is ever the restorer! It brings them back.

TURN WITH URGENCY

The New King James Version translates the first words of verse 12 in this way: '"Now, therefore," says the LORD.'

It is a statement of urgency. The New International Version

conveys it even better with these words: '"Even now," declares the LORD.'

Repentance was of such vital importance that the people were to unite around it and give it priority.

The priests were to call for a solemn assembly. They were to gather the people (vv. 15–16). And the people were to come. They were not to let anything else have priority over this!

Old people were not to let the sicknesses and infirmities of their old age keep them away!

The parents were to make sure their children were there— even those that were still nursing!

The parents were not to allow their children to keep them or anyone else away. They were to bring the children! What does this passage have to say to those who believe that the only time their children should be in church is when there is something especially for them?

And the young couple who were getting ready for their marriage ceremony were to drop what they were doing and come to the solemn assembly. They were to stop dressing for their wedding and run to the solemn assembly to join in the repentance. This was the Lord's way of saying that those who have other pressing concerns should not allow those concerns to crowd out the main concern.

The priests themselves were to feel the urgency of the matter. They were not to wait until they got to the altar to weep, but were to weep while they were on the way (v. 17)!

Duane A. Garrett says that the repentance 'demanded a cessation of all normal activity'.[2]

Joel speaks very pointedly to us if we care to listen! He is putting his finger on one of the greatest problems of our day—getting God's people to lay down other things and give priority to getting right with God.

It has become very difficult for spiritual leaders to do what this passage says—gather the people. We try, but we have little success. We give plenty of notice. We say we are going to set a certain time for the people of God to give priority to the things of God; but this one says she must visit relatives, and that one over there says his children have a school activity or a sporting event.

Many church leaders have had so little success and so much disappointment in trying to gather the people that they have long since given up even trying. Others have determined that the only way the church can gather a party-mad people is by throwing a bigger party! Someone has observed that it is virtually impossible to get people together when God is the only attraction!

Church people always say to church leaders, 'You must pick a convenient time to gather the people.' And God says to church people, 'You must lay aside those things that make the time inconvenient.'

Reflect on these points

1. When we read of God sending calamities upon his

people, we are inclined to think ill of him. But Joel gives us a beautiful picture of God: the picture of a father who, having disciplined his son, scoops him up in his arms, sets him on his lap and, with tender words, tells him how he can avoid such discipline in the future.

2. *Is it possible that the Lord is drawing a picture for us? The people have stopped following God. It is the duty of every child of God to get behind God and follow him, but we cannot follow sin and follow God. When we repent and get behind God, he starts leading us again.*

3. *Joel is putting his finger on one of the greatest problems of our day—getting God's people to lay down other things and give priority to getting right with God.*

The Prophet
Amos

Our hope-giving God

'On that day I will raise up The tabernacle of David, which has fallen down, and repair its damages; I will raise up its ruins, and rebuild it as in the days of old;

That they may possess the remnant of Edom, and all the Gentiles who are called by My name,' says the LORD who does this thing.

'Behold, the days are coming,' says the LORD, 'when the plowman shall overtake the reaper, and the treader of grapes him who sows seed; the mountains shall drip with sweet wine, and all the hills shall flow with it.

I will bring back the captives of My people Israel; they shall build the waste cities and inhabit them; they shall plant vineyards and drink wine from them; they shall also make gardens and eat fruit from them.

I will plant them in their land, and no longer shall they be pulled up from the land I have given them,' says the LORD your God.

Amos 9:11–15

Although he was from the kingdom of Judah, Amos was called to preach to the neighbouring kingdom of Israel.

And he seemed to be out of his mind for doing so! Things were going so well in Israel! It was a boom time! Money was plentiful, and religion was flourishing.

But Amos could see beneath the façade some things that were hidden from the people in general, things such as corruption, greed, oppression of the poor, religious formalism, idolatry, immorality and disdain for authority.

And Amos did not hesitate to call these things to the

attention of the people of Israel and to tell the people that they could not possibly get away with them. God's judgement was brewing and would soon be poured out upon them.

The Minor Prophets have often been misrepresented. Because they so emphatically declared the judgement of God on human wickedness, they have been regarded as negative and narrow men—men of one note, and a harsh one at that!

But these men never failed to include in their prophecies the note of hope. They were balanced men.

What a heart-warming note of hope we have at the end of Amos' prophecy! These words do not come from Amos; they come through him from the hope-giving God. The Lord caused Amos to lift up his eyes from the dark times in which he was living to look to a better day. As Amos looked towards that better day, he could not help but be flooded with hope, and, in these closing verses, he asks the people of Israel to join him in looking towards that better day and in sharing that hope.

As we examine these words, we can identify five reasons for hope.

God promises a king (v. 11)

The Lord says, 'On that day I will raise up the tabernacle of David, which has fallen down …'

The house of David was in a very sad and deplorable state at this time. The very fact that there were now two kingdoms, Judah and Israel, instead of one, tells us that David's house had fallen on hard times. Yes, the descendants of David were still ruling over the kingdom of Judah, but they were nothing like David.

David's descendants did not measure up to their ancestor, and the immediate future was even bleaker for the house of David. The kingdom of Judah would eventually be destroyed, and it looked for a while as if the house of David would be as well.

What is so important about that? It is that God had promised David an enduring house. In other words, God had promised to give David's house an everlasting kingdom (2 Sam. 7:13, 16).

In the verses of our text, Amos declared that the Lord was going to keep that promise. And keep it he did! God sent the Lord Jesus, a descendant of David, and the Lord Jesus is the everlasting King who heads up an everlasting kingdom. Matthew Henry writes of Jesus: 'In him God's covenant with David had its accomplishment; and the glory of that house, which was not only sullied, but quite sunk, revived again ...'[1]

That brings us to a second reason for hope.

God promises victory (v. 12)

The Lord Jesus would not come merely to carry the banner of David forward, but as a mighty King to conquer and to lead his people to victory.

Amos makes reference to the people of God possessing 'the remnant of Edom' and 'all the Gentiles' who are called by his name.

He is telling us that the kingdom of Christ will be a successful kingdom.

The people of Israel had no greater enemy than Edom. She was Israel's bitter and intransigent foe. The prophecy that Israel would eventually possess Edom was, then, a promise that the Messiah's kingdom would finally crush even the bitterest opposition.

The kingdom of Jesus would also prove to be successful in another way. It would not be a kingdom of Jews only, but would also include God's chosen Gentiles.

We are living in days which make it appear as if the kingdom of Christ is fading and will soon be gone. Don't ever believe it. The kingdom of Christ will finally hold universal sway, even to the point that every knee will bow before Jesus and every tongue will confess that he is Lord of all.

Yet another reason for hope is this:

God promises plenty (v. 13)

This is pictured for us in a vivid and gripping way. The promised abundance will be of such a nature that the reaper will not be through with his work when the sower is ready to plant the next crop!

Since the other parts of this passage have to do with the coming of Jesus and his kingdom, we must understand this promise in that light as well. What, then, are we to conclude about the kingdom of Christ from this promise? One thing is that the preaching of the gospel will meet with success, as we noted.

But the larger thing is that the Lord Jesus will eventually

usher his people into a new earth. There the curse of sin will be for ever lifted (Rev. 22:3).

The abundance of the earth now is limited because creation is under the curse of sin, but when that curse is lifted, the abundance will be unspeakably great.

A fourth note of hope is this:

God promises satisfaction (v. 14)

The Lord assures his people that they would build houses and inhabit them, plant vineyards and drink the wine, and plant gardens and eat the produce.

This is a picture of satisfaction and fulfilment. There is no satisfaction in building a house and not being able to live in it. That is frustration and disillusionment. The same is true of planting a vineyard or a garden and not being able to enjoy the results.

So God was promising a day of satisfaction. To what day was he referring? Some take it to be the day when the people of Israel were finally released from the captivity that took them to a foreign land; but that was only a partial fulfilment. The final fulfilment will come in eternal glory, where the people of God will find complete satisfaction. They will never again be disillusioned or frustrated.

The final ground of hope is this:

God promises security (v. 15)

The Lord promises to plant his people in his land in such a way that they will never again be 'pulled up'.

Once again, we must look to eternal glory for the true fulfilment of this promise. There is no real security in this life. Our goods can be stolen; our health can fail; our friends can forsake us; our family members and friends can and do die; and we ourselves will finally die.

But when King Jesus takes his people home, they will be placed beyond all of these things for all time. There they will enjoy perfect security.

Let us never forget that all that God promises regarding eternal glory rests entirely on the Lord Jesus Christ and what he did on the cross. We owe all to him. Should we not be filling our lives with worshipping and serving him?

Reflect on these points

1. *We are living in days which make it appear as if the kingdom of Christ is fading and will soon be gone. But the kingdom of Christ will finally hold universal sway, and every knee will bow before Jesus and every tongue confess that he is Lord of all.*

2. *God was promising a day of satisfaction. The final fulfilment of that will come in eternal glory, where the people of God will find complete satisfaction. They will never again be disillusioned or frustrated.*

3. *There is no real security in this life. Our goods can be stolen; our health can fail; our friends can forsake us; our family members and friends can and do die; and we ourselves will finally die. But when King Jesus takes his*

people home, they will be placed beyond all of these things for all time. There they will enjoy perfect security.

The Prophet
Obadiah

Our triumphant God

'Though you ascend as high as the eagle, and though you set your nest among the stars, from there I will bring you down,' says the LORD.

'But on Mount Zion there shall be deliverance, and there shall be holiness; the house of Jacob shall possess their possessions.'

Then saviors shall come to Mount Zion to judge the mountains of Esau, and the kingdom shall be the LORD's.

Obadiah 4, 17, 21

We come now to the most minor of the minor! Obadiah is the shortest of the Minor Prophets, and, for that matter the shortest in the Old Testament.

I cannot tell you much about the prophet named Obadiah. I can tell you that his name means 'servant of the Lord' or 'worshipper of the Lord'.

As we look at Obadiah's little prophecy, we see that it has to do with the nation of Edom. The Edomites were the descendants of Esau, who was, of course, the brother of Jacob, who was the father of the twelve men after whom the twelve tribes of Israel were named.

It is doubtful that Obadiah actually went to Edom to declare the message. If he had done so, he would not have lived to tell the story! It is more likely that he delivered this message about Edom to his own people in Judah. It was a message 'concerning Edom' (v. 1).

I want to tell you a story, and after my story is over, you will see why the people of Judah would be very much interested in what Obadiah had to say about Edom.

The year is 586 BC. The nation of Judah is reeling. She is in terrible trouble. The Babylonians have come against her in mighty force intending to destroy the city of Jerusalem, including its beautiful temple, and to carry most of her citizens away to Babylon.

The people of Judah need help, but there is no help to be found from her neighbouring nation, Edom, although the Edomites and the Jews share the same blood.

We can go further. The people of Edom are not content merely to stand by while the Babylonians attack Judah. That would be bad enough. But they actually rejoice in Babylon's invasion of Judah. And they, the Edomites, even use the opportunity to loot Judah.

It gets worse. When some of the people from Judah try to escape from the Babylonians, the Edomites seize them and sell them into slavery (vv. 12–14).

Now we are in a position to see why Obadiah's message would be of interest to the people of Judah.

Edom's rejoicing over this calamity put the people of Judah in quite a dilemma. Why would God bring such severe judgement upon his own people and seemingly let a nation like Edom get away with wickedness?

We suddenly realize that this little prophecy is of paramount importance. It deals with an issue which confronts us quite as much as it did the people of Judah. We can put that issue in this way: Where is God when evil abounds? Or we can put it another way: Has evil defeated God?

We ourselves live in a day of abounding evil. Edomites are to be found on every hand—disregarding God, flaunting his laws and taunting his people. Does God know? Does he care?

Obadiah gives some very clear and emphatic answers to such questions.

God is going to judge evildoers (v. 4)

I have described the despicable things that the people of Edom did when Judah was invaded. I have not told you that Edom coupled with her hateful actions a very prideful attitude.

Edom was situated in a mountainous region. This made it very difficult for enemies to attack her, and this caused her to be very proud and very sure of herself (v. 3).

But Edom was not beyond the reach of God. So we read: '"I will bring you down," says the LORD' (v. 4).

We are living in a time of self-assured Edomites. They have taken their refuge in high places. The message of God is proclaimed, and they look down from their loftiness and say, 'No one believes like that any more.'

They point to the cross of Christ and tell us it is absurd for anyone to suggest that a Jew dying on a Roman cross over 2,000 years ago is the way of eternal salvation.

We could go on and on about what people today say from their lofty heights of intellectual pride and popular opinion. But what ultimately matters is not what they say, but what

God says. And God says to all those who are proud and who think they know more than he: 'I will bring you down!'

We can find another example of this with Belshazzar in the book of Daniel. Belshazzar was very proud and sure of himself, but God brought his kingdom to an end. And Daniel gave him the reason in these words: '... the God who holds your breath in His hand and owns all your ways, you have not glorified' (Dan. 5:23).

The prophecy of Obadiah reminds us that, although wicked people seem to be getting away with their wickedness, they really aren't. No one ever gets away with wickedness. Sooner or later, God will step in and balance the books. The *New Geneva Study Bible* says, 'When the church suffers at the hands of God's enemies, she needs to return to the prophecy of Obadiah and renew her faith in the just God revealed there. He cares for His persecuted people, and behind their present circumstances He is always at work for them.'[1]

God is going to save his people (v. 17)

God also had a word of comfort for his people. Yes, they experienced some terrible things. The Babylonians did carry out their plans against Judah. They did destroy Jerusalem, and they did carry most of the people away captive. And, yes, the people of Edom laughed and looted.

But this would not be the end of Judah. God says, 'But on Mount Zion there shall be deliverance' (v. 17).

'Zion' is another name for Jerusalem and another name for the people of God.

God was promising that Judah would be delivered from captivity and would be brought back to her land. He said that she would once again possess her possessions. The evil that Edom would do against Judah would not destroy her. She would be brought back and would triumph over it.

This is a marvellous picture of what God has in mind for all of his people of all ages. All of God's people are referred to as having come to 'Mount Zion' (Heb. 12:22), and on Mount Zion, they will all find deliverance.

God's people are often troubled, vexed and bewildered by the evils of this world, but there is coming a day when God will bring them to his heavenly Zion, and there evil will never be able to harm them again.

Let us make sure we understand that the deliverance that God's people will finally experience in glory will be due to the deliverance that they experience in this world: that is, deliverance from sin and condemnation on the basis of the redeeming death of Jesus on the cross. Those who are saved through Christ are delivered now and will be delivered even more finally in eternity.

God is going to rule over all (v. 21)

Obadiah wraps up his prophecy by speaking of a time when 'saviours' would come to Mount Zion. This is undoubtedly a reference to those who would return from captivity in Babylon.

When the people of Judah were carried away captive, the Edomites rejoiced because they thought that that would be the end of Judah; that she had ceased to exist as a nation and would never exist again. Those who would return from captivity would be 'saviours' in this sense: they would save Judah from extinction as a nation. They would be the means through which Judah was once again constituted a nation.

But there is more. Those returning captives would make it apparent to all that God had not abandoned his people, that he was still ruling over them.

We have here yet another picture of the end of time. As we have seen, the end will bring deliverance from evil for all the people of God. But it will also mean the end of all kingdoms except one!

It often appears now that the rule of God is hanging by a thread. Evil often seems to be flourishing, and God's cause failing.

But appearances are deceiving. When the end comes, we will see that God's rule was never in doubt. And we will understand that, even when evil appeared to be winning, God was merely using it to achieve his purpose. And on that day, when we lift up our eyes, all we will be able to see will be the kingdom of God. Then we will rejoice in knowing that 'The kingdoms of this world have become the kingdoms of our Lord and of His Christ' (Rev. 11:15).

The theologian Francis Schaeffer made this question famous: 'How should we then live?'

This is a good question for us to ponder. We have seen that our God is going to judge evil-doers, deliver his people and rule over all. How should we then live? We should make sure that we have received the deliverance that God now gives through Christ. And we should make sure that we do not allow ourselves to get discouraged. Yes, there is evil on every hand. But God has it on a short leash and will eventually bring it to a final and dramatic halt. Let us be looking forward to that day. Let us live with the spirit of triumph. Let us frequently remind ourselves that we have read the last chapter of the book, and God wins!

Reflect on these points

1. *We are living in a time of self-assured Edomites. They look down from their loftiness and say, 'No one believes like that any more.' But God says to all those who are proud and who think they know more than he: 'I will bring you down!'*

2. *God's people are often troubled by the evils of this world, but a day is coming when God will bring them to his heavenly Zion, and there evil will never be able to harm them again.*

3. *It often appears now that the rule of God is hanging by a thread. Evil often seems to be flourishing, and God's cause failing. But appearances are deceiving. When the end comes, we will see that God's rule was never in doubt. And on that day, when we lift up our eyes, all we will be able to see will be the kingdom of God. Then we will rejoice.*

The Prophet Jonah

Our compassionate God

Then God said to Jonah, 'Is it right for you to be angry about the plant?' And he said, 'It is right for me to be angry, even to death!'

But the LORD said, 'You have had pity on the plant for which you have not labored, nor made it grow, which came up in a night and perished in a night.

And should I not pity Nineveh, that great city, in which are more than one hundred and twenty thousand persons who cannot discern between their right hand and their left—and much livestock?'

Jonah 4:9–11

To be compassionate is to be tender, merciful or kind. It is to show sympathy or pity.

Our world aches for compassion.

One of the very best things I can tell you about our God is that he is compassionate. He is our compassionate God.

We can find this truth in many, many passages of Scripture, but it never shines more brilliantly than in the little prophecy of Jonah. Jonah is a study in God's compassion.

The prophecy offers us two examples of God granting compassion to pagans. Both Jonah's shipmates and the people of Nineveh come to true faith in God!

But we are primarily interested in the compassion the Lord showed to the prophet himself. We can identify four major expressions of God's compassion to his reluctant prophet, some of which do not at first glance seem to be very compassionate at all.

The compassion of the tossed ship and the gulping fish (1:1–17)

The prophecy begins with our compassionate God determining to show mercy to the Ninevites. He was going to send Jonah to preach to them. God has no greater mercy to show than the mercy of granting people his Word!

But there was a problem. Jonah did not want the Ninevites to hear the Word of God. If they heard it, they might believe and turn from their sins. If they turned from their sins while Jonah's own nation, Israel, was refusing to do the same, God might cut Israel off and replace her with the Ninevites.

To protect his people, Jonah ran from God. O. Palmer Robertson says that Jonah 'would rather see the heathen Ninevites perish than see the disobedient Israelites perish'.[1]

Jonah ran down to Joppa, down to a ship sailing to Tarshish, down into the hold of that ship. And there in the silence and isolation of that hold, Jonah thought he had escaped. But he had not. Robertson writes, 'Trying to get away from God is like trying to get away from air.'[2]

The God from whom Jonah ran was in full pursuit. He commanded 'a great wind' to create 'a mighty tempest on the sea'. That tempest was so great 'that the ship was about to be broken up' (v. 4).

The terror-stricken sailors roused Jonah from his sleep, brought him on deck, and, through the casting of lots, ascertained that he was the cause of the storm. Some would call this an amazing coincidence, but in God's world, there are no coincidences, only providences.

These sailors then threw Jonah overboard, and the same Lord who controlled the wind and the casting of the lots was not caught off guard. Waiting there in the water for the disobedient prophet was his own private ocean liner: a great fish (v. 17). One gulp and Jonah, who went down to Joppa, down to the ship, down to the hold, was further down than he ever thought he could go.

Let's not focus so much on the fish that we fail to focus on the God of the fish. The great fish must not obscure the great God!

Tossed by a storm and swallowed by a fish! These seem to be manifestations of God's anger instead of his compassion.

But let's answer some questions. When doctors diagnose and treat illnesses, are they being kind or cruel to their patients? When parents correct children, are they being kind or cruel to those children?

Doctors sometimes use unpleasant measures in order to achieve good for their patients. It is the same with parents and their children. And it is the same with God! He sent both the storm and the fish, not to be cruel to Jonah, but rather to be good to him. Do we agree that the happiness of the child of God lies in obedience to God? We must, then, agree with this: if God uses something to bring us to obedience, he is being good to us!

The author of Hebrews tells us that the Lord chastises his children. He writes, 'Now no chastening seems to be joyful for the present, but painful; nevertheless, afterward it yields the peaceable fruit of righteousness to those who have been trained by it' (Heb. 12:11).

Jonah himself said, 'Those who regard worthless idols forsake their own Mercy' (2:8).

He had made an idol out of his own selfish desires, and, in the belly of the fish, he realized what a fool he had been. If forsaking God is forsaking mercy, anything that brings us back to God is a mercy.

The compassion of the vomiting fish (2:10–4:4)

We have no trouble seeing God's compassion in the next part of the story. After spending three days and nights in the belly of the fish, Jonah was vomited 'onto dry land'.

The God who had chastised him with the storm and the fish now delivered him.

As we have noted, God does chastise his people, but his chastisement is not permanent. It is designed for their good and, when that good is achieved, God lifts the chastisement.

Our chastisement is always a vomiting fish. It is not permanent. It lasts only until its purpose is achieved, and then it ends.

Chastisement certainly achieved its purpose with Jonah. He went to Nineveh and began to preach, and, wonder of wonders, the people of Nineveh began to repent.

And our compassionate God 'relented from the disaster' that he had been planning to bring upon the Ninevites (3:10).

We might be inclined to think that Jonah would be pleased about the amazing response to his preaching, but he was far from it: 'But it displeased Jonah exceedingly, and he became angry' (4:1).

His reason for being angry at this point was the same as his reason for running from God. For years and years, God had been calling Israel to repent, and she refused. Yet the Ninevites began repenting on the first day of Jonah's preaching. Jonah could not help but conclude that the spiritual centre of gravity was shifting! God was turning away from the people of Israel to the Gentiles!

We could certainly understand it if God had washed his hands of Jonah at this point. Jonah prayed to die (4:3), and it would not surprise us if God complied!

But God, who is ever gracious and patient, once more expressed compassion.

The compassion of the gnawing worm (4:5–11)

Jonah had stationed himself outside the city of Nineveh to see what would happen. It was very hot out there! But the Lord 'prepared a plant and made it come up over Jonah, that it might be shade for his head, to deliver him from his misery' (v. 6).

Jonah was very happy about that plant (v. 6), but his happiness did not last long. A worm 'so damaged the plant that it withered' (v. 7).

The plant was gone and a 'vehement east wind' began to blow. And the sun was beating down. In his misery, Jonah once more expressed his desire to die (v. 8).

Jonah was obviously a very miserable and unhappy man, and the Lord had used the worm to make him that way. So we are faced with the same question about the worm that we asked about the storm and the great fish. Was the Lord being compassionate to Jonah in sending this worm?

Our answer must be the same. Yes, God was being compassionate. The worm was another form of chastisement. With the storm and the fish, God was bringing adversity into Jonah's life. With the worm, God was depriving him of blessing.

God still uses both forms of chastisement, and both forms are for our good.

The Lord responded to Jonah's desire to die by offering a shattering word. Jonah had felt pity for something that was of very little value—a plant. But he did not want God to show pity for eternal souls!

Are we willing to face this divine logic? Most of us care for houses, cars, plants and animals to the point that we are distressed if anything happens to them. Have we transferred that compassion to sinful people? Are we more concerned about a dent in our new car than we are about Christless souls going off into eternity?

Jonah does not tell us how he responded to the Lord's question in verse 11. Perhaps he ended his book with the question hanging there so that we will be forced to answer it ourselves.

In short, the option before each of us is to be like Jonah or to be like Jesus. Jonah grieved over a repentant city that had to be spared, while Jesus grieved over an unrepentant city that had to be judged (Matt. 23:37–39). Jonah lamented that his surrender to God had led to the salvation of pagans. Jesus lamented that the surrender of his own blood would not bring about the salvation of most in Jerusalem.[3]

Reflect on these points

1. *Doctors sometimes use unpleasant measures in order to achieve good for their patients. It is the same with God!*

2. *Do we agree that the happiness of the child of God lies in obedience to God? We must, then, agree with this: if God uses something to bring us to obedience, he is being good to us!*

3. *Most of us care for houses, cars, plants and animals to the point that we are distressed if anything happens to them. But are we more concerned about a dent in our new car than we are about Christless souls going off into eternity?*

4. *The option before us is to be like Jonah or to be like Jesus: Jonah grieved over a repentant city that had to be spared; Jesus grieved over an unrepentant city that had to be judged.*

The Prophet
Micah

Our pardoning God

Who is a God like You, pardoning iniquity and passing over the transgression of the remnant of His heritage? He does not retain His anger forever, because He delights in mercy.

He will again have compassion on us, and will subdue our iniquities. You will cast all our sins into the depths of the sea.

You will give truth to Jacob and mercy to Abraham, which You have sworn to our fathers from days of old.

Micah 7:18–20

Have you ever done something that you deeply regret? I am talking about something so horribly wrong that the mere remembrance of it makes you feel sick.

Do you sometimes find yourself thinking that you can never again be useful to the Lord because of the shameful thing you did?

Have you ever found yourself wishing that you could go back to that time when you made that terrible choice so that you could make the opposite choice?

We know that King David in the Old Testament reached a point where he would have given anything to have been able to push a rewind button and go back to that moment when he stood on his roof and noticed Bathsheba (2 Sam. 11:2–5).

And Simon Peter in the New Testament came to a point where he would have gladly given all to push a rewind button and go back to that sorrowful night when he stood by the fire with the enemies of Jesus (John 18:15–18, 25–27).

The same thing could be said of the people to whom Micah

prophesied—the people of Judah during the years 739 to 686 BC. These people had made some terrible choices, and they and their descendants would suffer some terrible consequences.

What were their choices? Micah leaves no doubt about them. He accuses the people of idolatry (1:7; 6:16), covetousness (2:2), oppression (2:2) and violence (2:2; 3:10; 6:12; 7:2). And he charges the leaders with disregard for justice (3:1–3, 9–10), hating good and loving evil (3:2), oppression of the poor (3:2b–3), obsession with money (3:11a) and with a presumptuous attitude that assumed that God would not judge (3:11b).

And what were the terrible consequences of their choices? The Babylonians would come in, destroy their homes, their cities and their temple, and would take most of the people into captivity.

When the full force of those consequences hit, those people would sorely regret the course they had chosen. They also would gladly be able to push the rewind button to go to that point where they had first begun to go astray.

But there was no rewind button for them to push. There was, however, something that those people could do! They could find pardon and forgiveness from God.

Filled with the Spirit of God, Micah was enabled to peer down the corridor of time to see his people sitting there in Babylon. And as they sat there in their misery and woe, he could hear them saying these words:

Do not rejoice over me, my enemy;

When I fall, I will arise;

When I sit in darkness,

The LORD will be a light to me.

I will bear the indignation of the LORD,

Because I have sinned against Him,

Until He pleads my case

And executes justice for me;

He will bring me forth to the light;

I will see His righteousness.

(7:8–9)

There is no rewind button for our lives, either! We cannot go back, no matter how fervently we may wish we could.

But we too can find pardon from God. This is a wonderful thing, far too wonderful for words! Let's raise, and seek to answer, some vital questions about God's pardon.

What does God do with our sins?

PARDONS (V. 18)

First, he pardons them. The word translated 'pardon' means 'lift up' or 'take away'.

Sin is a heavy burden that weighs us down and causes us to fall. God lifts it and takes it away so that it will never burden us again.

God also passes over our sin. Sin is a foul, repulsive thing, but God takes no notice of it.

We will realize that this is no small thing only if we

understand the foul nature of sin. Micah drives this home to our hearts by using three words for sin.

The first is 'iniquity', which suggests twistedness, crookedness or perversity.

We are by nature 'twisters'. We take God's good gifts and use them in ways in which they were never meant to be used. We twist them. The people of Judah were doing this. They were making the rightful desire to have sufficient material possessions into an obsession with such things. Micah says that covetousness had such a powerful grip on the people of Judah that they could not get away from it when they went to bed. Their beds had become places of unrest instead of places of rest. While the people were lying in their beds, their minds were churning with ways in which they could seize property. When morning came, they wasted no time in leaping out of their beds to put their schemes into action (2:1).

The second word is 'transgression'. This word conveys the idea of going aside. God's law is the path which we should follow, but we deviate or go aside from it and walk in our own way. To transgress, then, is to rebel against God's way.

The final word Micah uses is 'sins' (v. 19). To sin is to miss or fall short of the mark or standard that God has set for us.

The common denominator with each of these words is an objective standard. Something is straight, but we twist it. There is a way, but we refuse to walk in it. There is a target, but we miss it.

And all of this applies to us just as much as it did to Micah's generation!

SUBDUES (v. 19)

God also subdues our sin. It is an enemy that is too strong for us, but God defeats it. John Gill describes this part of God's dealing with the sins of his people in this way: '... God tramples upon it, as a conqueror does upon the necks of his enemies; it is subdued by him, and is under his feet; which he treats with contempt, disdains to look upon, keeps it under, so that it shall never rise again to the condemnation of his people ...'[1]

CASTS (v. 19)

Finally, God casts 'all our sins into the depths of the sea'.

All of the statements that Micah makes about God's dealings with our sins are very precious indeed, but none is more so than this one. Think of it! God casting our sins into the depths of the sea! Kenneth L. Barker writes, '... just as the Lord hurled Pharaoh's chariots and his army into the sea and they sank to the depths like a stone (Exod 15:4–5), so he will hurl all "our" sins into the depths of the sea. This, of course, speaks of the complete forgiveness of sin and the removal of its guilt forever (see Jer 50:20).'[2]

Barker then cites the *New International Version Study Bible*: 'God not only puts our sins out of sight (Isa 38:17); he also puts them out of reach (Mic 7:19; Ps 103:12), out of mind (Jer 31:34), and out of existence (Isa 43:25; 44:22; Ps 51:1, 9; Acts 3:19).'[3]

This is the sea of God's forgetfulness. For God to cast our

sins there means that he not only forgives them, but he also forgets them. As far as he is concerned they are gone, and gone forever. You can keep fish forever in this sea and never reel in one sin that has been forgiven by God.

But if God casts our sins into the sea, why do we still remember them and why are we still haunted by them? We must remember that the sea into which they are cast is God's forgetfulness! God does not remember them, but the devil makes sure that we do. He would never dare fish in the sea of God's forgetfulness. He knows he can catch nothing there! But he does fish in the sea of our remembrance, and, sure enough, he catches lots of fish there!

We must make it our business to resist the devil, and, when he brings a forgiven sin to mind, we must tell him that God has forgotten it. Point him to the grace of God, and he will flee.

How does God do these things?

The things God does with our sins are breathtaking indeed. But they do raise a question that must be answered. We know that God is holy, and yet here we have Micah telling us that God pardons, passes over, subdues and casts our sins into the depths of the sea.

God's holiness requires him to judge sin. Take this matter of God passing over our sin: How can God do this when his holiness requires him to judge it? How can he take no notice of our sin when his holy character requires him to take notice of it?

The answer to all such questions is the Lord Jesus Christ.

Yes, God's holy character requires him to judge sin, but his gracious character compels him to forgive sinners. The great throbbing question, then, is how can God satisfy both the demands of his justice and the demands of his grace? To put it another way: How can God at one and the same time carry out the penalty he has pronounced on sinners and let those very sinners go free?

As I said, the Lord Jesus is the answer. The Lord Jesus satisfied the demands both of God's justice and of his grace. Jesus went to the cross to receive the penalty for sin, and there the cup of God's wrath was poured out on him until there was not one drop left. And justice looked upon him dying there and said, 'I am satisfied.'

So it is that grace looked upon that same cross and said the same thing. You see, God's justice demands that the penalty for sin be paid, and even God himself cannot let sinners go free apart from that penalty being paid. But God demands that the penalty only be paid once, and, if Jesus paid it on my behalf, there is no penalty left for me.

But some will object that we have nothing in these verses from Micah about the Lord Jesus. And they will say that I am wrong for bringing him in! I will respond by saying that, while there may be nothing in the verses of our text about the Lord Jesus, we have no trouble finding him in Micah's prophecy (see 5:2–5a).

We can go further. Micah closes his prophecy by saying to the Lord:

> You will give truth to Jacob
> And mercy to Abraham,
> Which You have sworn to our fathers
> From days of old.

The people Micah was addressing were descendants of Abraham and Jacob. God took Abraham out of idolatry, sovereignly laying hold of him and making him his own, and God gave him the promise of the coming of the Messiah (Gen. 12:1–3). All of this was sheer mercy.

That which was mercy to Abraham was truth to Jacob. Once God promised it in mercy, it became truth upon which Jacob and all the rest of Abraham's descendants could depend. It is not that God's promise lost the quality of mercy when it came to Abraham's descendants; it is rather that, once it became a promise, it gained the quality of trustworthiness. God doesn't have to promise us anything: it is mercy when he does; but when he in mercy makes a promise, we can most certainly rely upon it.

In the Lord Jesus, God's mercy and truth met (Ps. 85:10). Jesus was both the gift of God's mercy and the fulfilment of God's promise.

But the point is this: in mentioning God's promises to Abraham and Jacob, Micah definitely had in mind the Messiah, through whom God pardons sinners.

Why does God do these things?

The answer is found in these words: 'He delights in mercy' (v. 18).

It would have been a tremendous thing if Micah had only said that God is merciful. That alone would be enough to set joy-bells ringing in the heart of the sinner who is miserably convinced of personal guilt before God. But Micah says something that is much stronger and much more glorious: God delights in mercy!

In his inimitable way, Charles Spurgeon said of the Lord,

> He delights in mercy, just as some men delight in trade, some in arts, some in professions; and each man, according to his delight, becomes proficient in pursuing a work for the very love thereof. So God is proficient in mercy. He addicts himself to it. He is most God-like, most happy, if such a thing may be said of him, when he is stretching out his right hand with his golden sceptre in it, and saying to the guilty, 'Come to me, touch this sceptre, and you shall live!'[4]

Here is the Lord's own testimony regarding the matter: '"For I have no pleasure in the death of one who dies," says the Lord GOD. "Therefore turn and live!"' (Ezek. 18:32).

What should our response be?

Micah himself leads the way for us, exclaiming: 'Who is a God like You, pardoning iniquity ...?'

We hear in his words a note of wonder and astonishment.

He is amazed that the holy God actually pardons sinners. He is obviously thrilled and captivated by God.

We are called to share his response, taking as our own these words:

> Great God of wonders! all thy ways
> Are matchless, Godlike and divine;
> But the fair glories of thy grace
> More Godlike and unrivalled shine.
> Who is a pardoning God like thee?
> Or who has grace so rich and free?
>
> (Samuel Davies)

Reflect on these points

1. *Sin is a heavy burden that weighs us down and causes us to fall. God lifts it and takes it away so that it will never burden us again.*

2. *For God to cast our sins 'into the depths of the sea' means that he not only forgives them, but he also forgets them. As far as he is concerned they are gone, and gone for ever.*

3. *God's justice demands that the penalty for sin be paid. But God demands that the penalty only be paid once, and, if Jesus paid it on my behalf, there is no penalty left for me.*

4. *God delights in mercy! 'He is most God-like, most happy ... when he is stretching out his right hand with his golden sceptre in it, and saying to the guilty, "Come to me, touch this sceptre, and you shall live!"'*

The Prophet
Nahum

Our good God

The LORD *is good, a stronghold in the day of trouble; and He knows those who trust in Him.*

But with an overflowing flood he will make an utter end of its place, and darkness will pursue His enemies.

Nahum 1:7–8

In approximately 760 BC, God sent the reluctant prophet Jonah to Nineveh, the capital city of the Assyrian Empire, to warn of impending judgement. The people of the city repented and were spared.

The spiritual awakening in Nineveh was deep and real, but, with the passing of time, the Ninevites returned to wickedness.

Once again, God had mercy upon the Ninevites. This time he sent the prophet Nahum to them. Nahum's message was the same as Jonah's. Because of their great wickedness, the Lord was planning to send catastrophic judgement upon them. This time, there was no repentance, and there was no escape. In 612 BC, the city of Nineveh fell to the Babylonians.

Nahum divided his message to the Ninevites into two parts: the nature of God (1:1–8) and the nature of the judgement God was planning to send (1:9–3:19).

We find our text in the first of these divisions. Nahum is describing the character of God. He is holy and just (vv. 2–3). He is longsuffering (v. 3). He is great in power (v. 3). And God is good (v. 7)!

Some think that Nahum has a contradiction on his hands. Reading what he has to say about God being holy and noting what he has to say about God's devastating judgement, they conclude that God is anything but good. A good God would never send such judgement! As far as they are concerned, God cannot be both just and good. He has to be one or the other. If he is just, he is mean and severe. If he is good, he does not judge. It has to be one way or the other!

Such people use a kind of logic on God that they do not employ in other areas of life. Here is a surgeon who cuts your loved one open and removes something! Is the doctor mean or good? We know the answer!

Sin is to the spiritual life what a cancerous tumour is to the physical life, and judgement is God's surgical knife by which he removes the sin. Is he good or cruel? If we say the surgeon is good, we must also say that God is good.

Think of it in terms of a judge. Here is a gang of young thugs who are terrorizing the community. They are beating people and stealing their goods. Finally, they are arrested and brought before the judge, who hears the case. The time has come for sentence, and the judge speaks: 'I know these boys have done terrible things, but I do not want to be mean or cruel to them. So I am going to release them without punishment.' Is the judge good or is he cruel?

A God who refuses to judge sin is not a good God!

One evidence of the Lord's goodness is this:

He is a stronghold in the day of trouble (v. 7)

We understand what Nahum's words meant to the people of that time. A stronghold was a fortified place, and the day of trouble was the day when the army of an enemy would approach. On that day, the people would run inside the stronghold. There they would be safe.

Nahum was telling them that the Lord was like that stronghold. They could come to him in times of distress, and he would help them.

Much has changed since this verse was written. Armies don't attack as they did in those days, and we do not have walled cities into which we can run.

But we do know about the day of trouble! And the good news is that the Lord is just as sufficient now for the day of trouble as he was so long ago.

I wonder if this is a day of trouble for you. Is it serious illness that is causing you trouble? Is it the death of a loved one? Is it conflict with family members or friends? Is it concern about the condition of the world and concern about the cause of Christ? Is it a strong, abiding sense of having failed the Lord?

There is no shortage of trouble-making circumstances! But there is good news for all God's people who are distressed in any way: the Lord is a stronghold. You can run to him! He may remove the trouble, or he may give you strength to face it. There is always help of some kind from the Lord!

There is no greater trouble in this entire world than the wrath of God, and the Bible tells us that we are all destined to face that wrath because of our sinful condition. But there is a stronghold into which we can run, a stronghold in which there is perfect protection from that trouble. That stronghold is the cross of Christ. Jesus went to that cross to receive the wrath of God in the place of sinners, and all who will flee to him will never have to experience that wrath themselves.

How very good it was of God to provide through his Son a perfect refuge in which we can be sheltered from his wrath! Do you find yourself looking at your difficult circumstances and wondering if God really is good? Look to the cross of Christ! That is the supreme expression of God's goodness, and, if God was willing to do the supreme thing for us, we must never doubt his goodness.

Another evidence of the Lord's goodness is this:

He knows those who trust in him (v. 7)

What riches we have in this statement! God knows his people!

He knew his people before the world began, and chose to make them his own!

The Lord Jesus knew the people of God when he died on the cross! The Bible tells us that he saw his seed and was satisfied (Isa. 53:10–11). It was the Lord Jesus who said, 'I am the good shepherd; and I know My sheep, and am known by My own' (John 10:14).

The Holy Spirit knew each of the people of God in time and granted spiritual life to them.

If you know the Lord, it is because he has known you. The apostle Paul refers to the Galatians knowing the Lord, but he then, as it were, catches himself. If I may paraphrase, Paul says to them, 'You Galatians have come to know God, but, to be perfectly accurate, you are known by God' (Gal. 4:9).

The knowledge God has of his people continues. Brother or sister in Christ, the God who has known you from eternity knows you now. He knows all about you. He has every hair of your head numbered. He knows every burden you carry. He knows every tear that falls from your eyes.

How thankful we should be for our knowing God!

But this word 'know', as Nahum uses it, means even more. Waylon Bailey writes, 'This "knowing" of the Lord must be understood in the full biblical sense of "loving" with the most intense care.'[1]

J. N. Heflin says, 'Knowledge in a biblical sense is not so much head knowledge, but heart knowledge; it refers to intimacy of relationship. To know someone is to have a meaningful relationship with him or her. It is because God intimately relates to His own that He provides care for them.'[2]

This is the God who tells us to cast our cares upon him because he cares for us (1 Peter 5:7).

This is the God who says to us,

> Fear not, for I have redeemed you;
> I have called you by your name;
> You are Mine.
> When you pass through the waters, I will be with you;
> And through the rivers, they shall not overflow you.
> When you walk through the fire, you shall not be burned,
> Nor shall the flame scorch you.
>
> (Isa. 43:1b–2)

This is the God who says to us,

> Can a woman forget her nursing child,
> And not have compassion on the son of her womb?
> Surely they may forget,
> Yet I will not forget you.
> See, I have inscribed you on the palms of My hands;
> Your walls are continually before Me.
>
> (Isa. 49:15–16)

Nahum's message is certainly one that we need. Our God is good! And, in his goodness, he shelters his people in their days of trouble and he knows them perfectly.

But we must know that these things are only true of those who trust the Lord, as our text so plainly declares.

So the most important business in this life is trusting the Lord.

Reflect on these points

1. *Is this a day of trouble for you? The Lord is a stronghold! You can run to him! He may remove the trouble, or he may give you strength to face it. There is always help of some kind from the Lord!*

2. *There is no greater trouble in this world than the wrath of God, and we are all destined to face that wrath because of our sinful condition. But there is a stronghold into which we can run: the cross of Christ.*

3. *Do you find yourself looking at your difficult circumstances and wondering if God really is good?*

Look to the cross of Christ! That is the supreme expression of God's goodness, and, if God was willing to do the supreme thing for us, we must never doubt his goodness.

4. *If you know the Lord, it is because he has known you. And the God who has known you from eternity knows you now. He knows all about you: every burden you carry and every tear that falls from your eyes. How thankful we should be for our knowing God!*

The Prophet
Habakkuk

Our joy-producing God

Though the fig tree may not blossom, nor fruit be on the vines; though the labor of the olive may fail, and the fields yield no food; though the flock may be cut off from the fold, and there be no herd in the stalls—

Yet I will rejoice in the LORD, I will joy in the God of my salvation.

The LORD God is my strength; he will make my feet like deer's feet, and He will make me walk on my high hills.

To the Chief Musician. With my stringed instruments.

Habakkuk 3:17–19

Here is a vital question for each of us to consider: Do we draw our happiness from our circumstances or from the Lord?

We can surely see the importance of this question. If we insist on finding our happiness in our circumstances, our lives will be like roller coasters. We will be happy one moment and sad the next. Why? Because our circumstances are constantly changing.

But if we find our happiness in the Lord, we will always be happy. The Lord never changes!

Habakkuk was a man who learnt to find his happiness in the Lord. I say 'learnt' because Habakkuk did not always do this. At the beginning of his prophecy, we find him down in the dumps. And the reason is not hard to find: he and his people were in the midst of horrible circumstances.

Habakkuk was a prophet to the nation of Judah just a few

years before the Babylonians came in to devastate the city of Jerusalem completely and carry most of the people into captivity.

The situation in which Habakkuk found himself caused him great consternation. He began by looking at the sinfulness of his people and wondering why God did not do something. As he looked around, he could easily see violence (1:2), iniquity, wickedness, strife and contention (1:3), lawlessness (1:4) and injustice (1:4).

God could surely set things right! Why didn't he?

By the way, the book of Habakkuk is unique in prophetic literature. The other books are primarily concerned with what the prophets said to their people and contain little of what transpired between the prophet and God. Habakkuk, on the other hand, contains nothing of what he said to the people but consists of what he and God said to each other (1:1–2:20) and the prophet's response to this dialogue (3:1–19).

The Lord had an answer for Habakkuk's question, but it wasn't the answer that the prophet wanted to hear. God said he was going to do something about the evil surrounding Habakkuk. God promised to 'work a work' (1:5) which the prophet would not have believed had someone other than God told him. This work would consist of God using the Babylonians as his instrument of judgement upon Judah.

Now Habakkuk has even more trouble on his hands! His nation is in the grip of iniquity, and God is going to correct it by using Babylon to destroy Judah! And Habakkuk is left to wonder how a holy God could use as his instrument of judgement a nation that is even more sinful than Judah (1:12–17).

So Habakkuk is not a happy man when we meet him. But look at the closing verses of his prophecy. Habakkuk has turned the corner! He says, 'Yet I will rejoice in the LORD, I will joy in the God of my salvation' (v. 18).

It is very important that we realize that Habakkuk's circumstances have not changed. His people are still very sinful, and the Babylonians are still coming!

The only thing that has changed is Habakkuk's perspective. He has come to see that he has reason to rejoice even when his circumstances are rotten. What is that reason? It is God himself!

Our reasons for happiness in God are always greater than our reasons for unhappiness (vv. 17–18)

Look at verse 17. It is a verse of problems, and the problems move from the lesser to the greater. They are in an 'ascending order of severity'.[1]

Habakkuk begins with the failure of the fig trees. Because figs were a delicacy, the loss of them was not all that serious.

The loss of grapes, which yielded drink for the people, was greater than the loss of figs. And the loss of the olives, the oil of which was used for cooking and lighting, was greater than the loss of grapes.

The greatest conceivable loss was that of 'the flock' (sheep) and the 'herd' (cattle). Waylon Bailey explains, 'Sheep and goats provided wool and the occasional meat for the Israelite diet. Hebrews did not normally eat cattle, but they were used for preparing the soil for planting and other heavy work.'[2]

Habakkuk is not saying that he will rejoice in God if he loses only a little. Rather, he is saying that he will rejoice in God even if he loses everything!

Now what would possess a man to say such a thing? Had Habakkuk lost his mind? No, not for a moment! As we examine his words, we find that he had good and solid reasons for rejoicing in God even in the midst of horrendous circumstances.

Our reasons for being happy in God are very great indeed (vv. 18–19)

One reason is simply this:

GOD IS GOD!

Look at the names the prophet uses for God. In verse 18, he calls him both 'LORD' and 'God', and in verse 19 he calls him 'the LORD God'.

Waylon Bailey maintains that Habakkuk used the strongest names available for God, names that 'emphasize the power and majesty of God'.[3]

If we have trouble delighting in God it is because we lack an adequate understanding of the glory of God. God is such a glorious being that he deserves our love and devotion even when our lives are difficult.

Just how great is our God? Habakkuk gives us an indication. We would say that God revealed his power on Mount Sinai when he gave the law to the nation of Israel (Exod. 19:16–25), but, surprisingly, Habakkuk says, 'there His power was hidden' (v. 4).

In everything he does, God keeps back more of his power than he uses. That is how great he is!

And, by the way, this glorious, sovereign God is the author of our circumstances. All circumstances, whether good or ill, come from his hand and from his heart of love for his people.

If the figs, the grapes, the olives, the flock and the herd fail, it is because God designed it to be so, and, if he designed it to be so, we can rest assured that God is achieving some purpose in our lives.

We can tell what our spiritual condition is by how we answer this question: Do we serve God because of what we can get out of him, or simply because he is God?

This is the issue in the book of Job. Satan suggested that the only reason any person ever serves God is for the blessings God gives him or her. Remove the blessings, and, at the same time, you will remove that person's devotion. Job was a test case on this issue. God allowed Satan to remove the external blessings Job had enjoyed, and it looked for a while as if Satan was going to win the point. Job's faith faltered, but then it rallied, and Job came out saying that he would love God even if God killed him (Job 13:15).

The Lord Jesus, as always, is an even greater example. He continued in faithful love and devotion to the Father even though it meant going to the cross. Why? Jesus perfectly understood that God is to be worshipped and served just because he is God.

A second reason Habakkuk was determined to rejoice in God in hard circumstances is this:

GOD IS THE GOD OF SALVATION

Look again at verse 18: 'Yet I will rejoice in the LORD, I will joy in the God of my salvation.'

Yes, there was such a thing as salvation in Old Testament times! Habakkuk and all the other saints of that era were saved from their sins through faith in the Christ who was yet to come.

Habakkuk understood something that we seem often to forget, namely, that salvation from sin and eternal destruction is a blessing of such magnitude that we should rejoice even if God never blessed us in any other way.

No matter what trial comes to the Christian, and no matter how much it hurts, he or she can always say, 'Thank God, I am saved, and because I am saved, these trials will soon be over, and I will be in eternal glory where there will be no more trials.'

Let us never be in doubt about how God saves his people. It is only through the Lord Jesus Christ and his death on the cross. That death was like no other. It involved Jesus receiving the wrath of God so that all who believe in him would never have to receive that wrath themselves. He bore it all so that they would never have to bear any of it.

GOD IS THE GIVER OF STRENGTH

The final reason Habakkuk gives for rejoicing in God is this: God gives strength for the trials (v. 19).

Although his circumstances were most trying and severe, Habakkuk was confident that the Lord would enable him to face them. He also gives us insight into one way in which God strengthens his people for their trials: he looks forward to that day when God will make their feet 'like deer's feet'. Deer are very sure-footed animals, and there is coming a day when God's people will stand with sure, unslipping feet on the mountain of victory.

Reflect on these points

1. *If we insist on finding our happiness in our circumstances, our lives will be like roller coasters. We will be happy one moment and sad the next, because our circumstances are constantly changing. But if we find our happiness in the Lord, we will always be happy. The Lord never changes!*

2. *This glorious, sovereign God is the author of our circumstances. All circumstances, whether good or ill, come from his hand and from his heart of love for his people.*

3. *Do we serve God because of what we can get out of him, or simply because he is God?*

4. *We seem often to forget that salvation from sin and eternal destruction is a blessing of such magnitude that we should rejoice even if God never blessed us in any other way.*

The Prophet Zephaniah

Our singing God[1]

The LORD *your God in your midst, the Mighty One, will save; he will rejoice over you with gladness, he will quiet you with His love, he will rejoice over you with singing.*

Zephaniah 3:17

The Bible is the account of God speaking. God spoke, and this world and the whole universe sprang into existence. As we work our way through the Old Testament, we consistently find God speaking. He spoke to Abraham and Moses, to Joshua and Gideon, to Samuel and David. We find God calling a steady succession of prophets to speak for him. We come to the New Testament and we find the Lord Jesus Christ stepping onto the stage of human history. The Lord Jesus came to speak the words of God, and he spoke in such a way that his listeners 'marveled at the gracious words which proceeded out of His mouth' (Luke 4:22).

We are very familiar, then, with God speaking. But here in Zephaniah we have the prophet promising his people that God would sing over them.

The prophecy of Zephaniah is built around two 'days'. The first is the terrible day of God's judgement upon the people of Judah (1:7, 14–16). That day would arrive when the Babylonians came in to devastate the nation and carry the people away captive.

The second day is the day of restoration when, after seventy years of captivity, the people would be released and brought back to their homeland. Zephaniah was looking at this day when he made reference to God singing.

These words are filled to the brim with breathtaking truths for the people of Judah, and for us as well. God's presence is here: he has promised to be in their midst. God's power is here: he, mighty to save, would deliver and protect his people. And God's enjoyment of his people is here: he would 'quiet' them with his love (perhaps meaning that he would quietly enjoy them as he rested in his love for them). He would rejoice over them with singing.

God singing! Let's explore this a bit.

Those over whom God promised to sing

A REPENTANT PEOPLE

The people of Judah would go into captivity in Babylon because of their sins. Zephaniah mentions in particular their idolatrous worship (1:4–6) and their moral degeneracy (3:1, 3–4). A good summary of the wickedness of the people is found in the four specific indictments of the second verse of chapter 3. The people of Judah refused to obey God, to receive correction, to trust God and to draw near to God.

At this time, the Lord did not sing over them, but grieved. In his grief, he sent them to Babylon. There they came to their senses and repented of their sins, and God began to rejoice over them. God always rejoices over his people, no matter how grievous their sin, if they will turn from those sins and give him the devotion he desires and deserves. Jesus' parable of

the prodigal son is a New Testament illustration of this truth
(Luke 15:11–24).

AN IMPERFECT PEOPLE

While the people of God repented in their captivity, they came
back to their homeland as an imperfect people. All we have to
do to see this is read the post-exilic prophets the Lord sent to
them: Haggai, Zechariah and Malachi.

But the prophecy of Zephaniah makes a wonderful truth
exceedingly plain: the Lord would sing over them even in their
imperfection.

Many Christians are keenly conscious of their failings. They
remember the determination they had when they first came to
know the Lord. They remember how eager they were to serve
him and how fervently they loved him. But, with the passing of
time, they found their ardour cooling. They now realize that
they have not been much in their Bibles or in prayer. They have
not had much concern over the souls of others. They may have
even engaged in a particularly heinous sin.

The truth is that many believers, if asked to convey how God
views them, would never think of him singing over them. They
would be more likely to regard him as a frowning, heavenly
policeman who is ready and eager to discipline them with his
celestial cudgel.

Let us be clear about this: while God does not excuse the
sins of his people, he still sees much in them that causes him
to rejoice. He sees in each of his children one for whom Christ
died, and he sings. He sees one in whom his Spirit operated,

and he sings. He sees one with whom his Spirit even now bears witness and for whom his Spirit prays, and he sings. He sees one who, with all his or her frailty and failings, loves him and desires to serve him, and he sings. He sees one who does not excuse sin but rather is troubled by it and desires to be free from it, and he sings. He sees one who is touched by the needs of others and desires to minister to them, and he sings. He sees one who, by his grace, will finally come into his presence to share his glory eternally, and he sings.

There is nothing in and of Christians themselves that makes God sing over them. But standing on the basis of the redeeming work of Christ and perfumed by Christ's ongoing ministry of intercession in heaven, each Christian is so pleasing to God that he, the Lord, bursts out in song. God does not sing over his people because they are worthy or deserving; he sings over them because they are tokens of his grace. His singing over his people testifies to his own grace that has worked in their lives, the grace that chose them, regenerated them, called them and forgave them. It is that grace that is now at work in sanctifying his people, and that grace will finally lead them home.

God the Father takes delight in God the Son. This was true before the foundation of the world; Paul tells us that 'All things were created ... for Him' (Col. 1:16). It was true while he was engaged in his earthly ministry, during which God spoke from heaven three times to express his delight (Matt. 3:17; 17:5; John 12:27–28). It is true now, in that the Lord Jesus Christ is now at the right hand of God to make intercession for all who believe (Mark 16:19; Rom. 8:34; Eph. 1:20; Col. 3:1).

If God so delights in his Son, he cannot help but delight in those who are covered by the righteousness of his Son.

The appropriate response to God's singing

JOY

Through the prophet, the Lord says,

> Sing, O daughter of Zion!
> Shout, O Israel!
> Be glad and rejoice with all your heart,
> O daughter of Jerusalem!
>
> (3:14)

If God is singing over his people, they have abundant reason to sing. They have reason to rejoice, not half-heartedly and casually, but whole-heartedly and fervently. Alexander Maclaren appropriately writes of this text,

> It becomes us to see to it that our religion is a religion of joy. Our text is an authoritative command as well as a joyful exhortation, and we do not fairly represent the facts of Christian faith if we do not 'rejoice in the Lord always.' In all the sadness and troubles which necessarily accompany us, as they do all men, we ought by the effort of faith to set the Lord always before us that we be not moved.[2]

> Let those refuse to sing
> Who never knew our God;
> But children of the heavenly King,
> But children of the heavenly King,
> May speak their joys abroad,
> May speak their joys abroad …
>
> Then let our songs abound,
> And every tear be dry;
> We're marching thro' Immanuel's ground,
> We're marching thro' Immanuel's ground,
> To fairer worlds on high,
> To fairer worlds on high.

(Isaac Watts)

CONFIDENCE

The Lord also says to his people,

> In that day it shall be said to Jerusalem:
> 'Do not fear;
> Zion, let not your hands be weak.'

(3:16)

The phrase 'let not your hands be weak' refers to letting the hands drop in fear and despair. The Lord wanted his people to understand that there was no reason for them to despair. Their sins had not separated them from him. He would still delight in them.

Believers today are entitled to draw comfort here. If the Lord has such delight in his people, we can be sure that he is aware of our circumstances and is present in the midst of them to sustain and help us. If God is delighted with his people, we can be sure that he will never throw his hands up in despair over us, but will finally complete his work in us and bring us to eternal glory. God will never allow himself to be deprived of one single believer, because each one brings him so much joy. Let the devil rage. If God is singing, the devil's rage doesn't matter.

Reflect on these points

1. *While God does not excuse the sins of his people, he still sees much in them that causes him to rejoice. He sees in each of his children one for whom Christ died, and he sings.*

2. *God does not sing over his people because they are worthy or deserving; he sings over them because they are tokens of his grace. His singing testifies to his grace that has chosen them, regenerated them, called them and forgiven them. That grace is now at work sanctifying his people, and it will finally lead them home.*

3. *If God is singing over his people, they have abundant reason to sing. They have reason to rejoice, not half-heartedly and casually, but whole-heartedly and fervently.*

4. *If the Lord has such delight in his people, we can be sure that he is aware of our circumstances and is present in the midst of them to sustain and help us. If God is delighted with his people, we can be sure that he will finally complete his work in us and bring us to eternal glory.*

The Prophet
Haggai

Our peace-giving God

For thus says the LORD *of hosts: 'Once more (it is a little while) I will shake heaven and earth, the sea and dry land;*

and I will shake all nations, and they shall come to the Desire of All Nations, and I will fill this temple with glory,' says the LORD *of hosts.*

'The silver is Mine, and the gold is Mine,' says the LORD *of hosts.*

'The glory of this latter temple shall be greater than the former,' says the LORD *of hosts. 'And in this place I will give peace,' says the* LORD *of hosts.*

Haggai 2:6–9

The book of Haggai brings us to the post-exilic prophets, that is, those prophets who ministered to the Jews who returned from captivity in Babylon. Haggai, whose name means 'festive', gives us a prophecy that is second only to Obadiah in terms of brevity.

The post-exilic Jews faced many challenges and hardships. Their homes and cities had to be rebuilt, as did the temple of God in Jerusalem.

The people did well for a while. In a burst of euphoria over their release, and out of gratitude to God for providing it, they set to work on the temple. But, as we all know from personal experience, we often have difficulty living up to the goals we set for ourselves. So it was with these people. They soon put aside work on the temple so that they could devote themselves to their own affairs (1:4).

For sixteen long years, the temple stood in an uncompleted

state, as the people busied themselves with other things. When they were confronted with their neglect of the temple, they would simply respond, 'The time has not come, the time that the LORD's house should be built' (1:2).

These people needed a good jolt, and God provided it for them through the ministry of Haggai. His prophecy consists entirely of four sermons that he delivered to the people. Each of these sermons begins with these words: 'the word of the LORD came by Haggai the prophet'.

We can characterize these sermons in this way: a sermon of rebuke (1:1–15), a sermon of encouragement (2:1–9), a sermon of rebuke and encouragement (2:10–19), and a sermon of encouragement (2:20–23).

The verses of our text are found in the second of these sermons. This sermon addresses one of the major reasons why the people had stopped working on the temple, namely, their awareness that it could not possibly match the beauty or glory of Solomon's temple. Anything they built would suffer by comparison. In relationship to Solomon's temple, the new would be 'as nothing' (2:3).

Haggai addressed this issue by offering the following encouragements to his people: (1) the same God who had been with Solomon would be with them (v. 5); (2) the absence of gold and silver in their temple would not mean anything to the Lord because he possesses all gold and silver (v. 8); (3) their temple would have greater glory than Solomon's because the Messiah himself would come to it (vv. 7, 9).

In promising the coming of the Messiah, the Lord spoke these words: 'And in this place I will give peace' (v. 9).

So God promised to give them peace. He was their peace-giving God, and he is ours as well.

He promised to give them peace in the temple, and he gives us peace in the same way. I am saying that the temple they were building was an emblem or a type of a far greater temple—the Lord Jesus Christ himself! And we find peace in him!

Jesus is the true temple of God

The temple was a physical manifestation of the truth that God dwells among his people (1 Kings 8:12–13; Ps. 132:13–14).

There can be no doubt, then, that Jesus is the true temple, because he was pre-eminently the one in whom God dwelt. The Gospel of John says of Jesus, 'And the Word became flesh and dwelt among us, and we beheld His glory, the glory as of the only begotten of the Father, full of grace and truth' (John 1:14).

Jesus dwelt among us, and God dwelt in him!

The apostle Paul put it succinctly: 'God was in Christ' (2 Cor. 5:19).

The Lord Jesus characterized himself as the temple of God. He called his body a temple (John 2:18–21). On another occasion, he referred to himself as 'One greater than the temple' (Matt. 12:6).

Jesus gives peace

We have established that Jesus is the true temple of God. He is the one in whom God fully and perfectly dwelt.

It is awesome to contemplate: Jesus was at one and the same time fully God and fully man. No one before him was in this category, and no one has been since. In all of human history, the Lord Jesus stands alone. He is unique—the God-man!

Have you ever wondered why he came? He certainly did not have to come. He did not have to take our flesh. There was no lack in him that our humanity could supply.

So why did he do it? He came because the God of peace desired to make peace with sinners. We can put it another way. Through Haggai, the Lord said of the temple, 'And in this place I will give peace' (v. 9). The Lord Jesus came so that God could keep that promise.

We must first understand that we are not naturally or automatically at peace with God. Quite the opposite! The Bible tells us that we all come into this world with a nature that is opposed to God, a nature that places us at odds with God.

No, it has not always been that way. Adam and Eve were at perfect peace with God until they disobeyed him. Their sin wrecked their peace with God. God created them for friendship with himself, but through sin they set the friendship of God aside and formed a friendship with the devil.

There is yet more. Because God determined that Adam would be the representative head of the whole human race, his sin constituted all of us sinners. We all come into this world, then, as friends of Satan rather than friends of God. We may not feel that we are enemies of God, but God says we are (Eph. 2:1–4).

God could have left us in this sorrowful condition. God could have spoken to us along these lines: 'You have chosen friendship with the devil, so friendship with him you will have.'

That would have meant eternal separation from God for all of us. That is where friendship with the devil leads.

Had God chosen to leave us as friends of Satan, we would have had no reason to complain. We have spurned his friendship. We have turned from him and spat upon him. He was under no obligation to do anything other than leave us to the consequences of our choice.

But in grace that is too great for us to comprehend, God determined that he would not let our friendship with Satan stand. He determined that he would break that friendship and restore all believers to friendship with himself.

There was only one way that this end could be accomplished. Because God is holy, he could not simply ignore our sin. His holiness requires him to judge sin, and God has judged it. He has pronounced eternal separation from himself as the penalty.

Even God himself cannot set that penalty aside. For him to do so would amount to him compromising his justice. If God were to ignore our sin, he would be guilty of sin himself.

So here was the piercing dilemma: How could God at one

and the same time make peace with sinners and carry out his penalty against them?

The Lord Jesus is the answer. He is the one through whom God makes peace. Jesus went to the cross to die a special kind of death. There he received the wrath of God against sinners. So the penalty has been paid! And because Jesus paid that penalty for all who will believe in him, there is no penalty left for them.

With sin out of the way, there is no longer any obstacle to the sinner having peace with God. By the blood of his cross, Jesus is the peacemaker.

The Spirit of God enabled Haggai to see the coming Christ and the peace that he would make. With this sight before him, Haggai called the Lord Jesus 'the Desire of All Nations' (v. 7).

What was Haggai saying? He was declaring Jesus to be the one who is desirable to all nations or the embodiment of all those things that every human heart desires. Jesus provides the peace for which we yearn, and only he can do so.

And with all this before him, Haggai promised his people that the temple they were building would have even greater glory than Solomon's. Let us learn from this that there is nothing more glorious than the saving gospel of Jesus through which God makes peace with sinners. And let us rejoice in that peace.

Reflect on these points

1. Jesus is the true temple of God. He is the one in whom

God fully and perfectly dwelt. It is awesome to contemplate: Jesus was at the same time fully God and fully man. He is unique—the God-man!

2. *We all come into this world as friends of Satan rather than friends of God. But in grace that is too great for us to comprehend, God determined that he would not let our friendship with Satan stand.*

3. *The Lord Jesus is the one through whom God makes peace. Jesus went to the cross and there received the wrath of God against sinners. Because Jesus paid that penalty for all who will believe in him, there is no penalty left for them.*

The Prophet
Zechariah

Our fountain-opening God

'In that day a fountain shall be opened for the house of David and for the inhabitants of Jerusalem, for sin and for uncleanness.

'It shall be in that day,' says the LORD of hosts, 'that I will cut off the names of the idols from the land, and they shall no longer be remembered. I will also cause the prophets and the unclean spirit to depart from the land.

It shall come to pass that if anyone still prophesies, then his father and mother who begot him will say to him, "You shall not live, because you have spoken lies in the name of the LORD." And his father and mother who begot him shall thrust him through when he prophesies.

'And it shall be in that day that every prophet will be ashamed of his vision when he prophesies; they will not wear a robe of coarse hair to deceive.

But he will say, "I am no prophet, I am a farmer; for a man taught me to keep cattle from my youth."

And one will say to him, "What are these wounds between your arms?" Then he will answer, "Those with which I was wounded in the house of my friends."'

Zechariah 13:1–6

An inexpressibly wonderful passage is this! Here we have the promise of a fountain opened for cleansing!

Physical cleansing is a welcome thing when we are covered with grime. Nothing is more welcome than slipping into a refreshing bath or shower after a long day of toiling in dirt and mire. But the cleansing promised here is not physical in nature. It is far greater than that.

The prophet Zechariah, whose name means 'God remembers', came on the scene to encourage the post-exilic Jews. He did so by urging them to keep their eyes peeled on a couple of things: their present duty and their future blessing.

Their present duty consisted of rebuilding the temple. Zechariah joined his contemporary, Haggai, in pressing this duty upon the people.

But Zechariah also had an eye to the future, and he wanted his people to have the same. We always find grace for the present by looking towards future blessing.

The future was bright indeed for the Jewish people. God had neither forgotten nor abandoned his promise to send the Messiah. How Zechariah loved to dwell on the promise of the Messiah! It is interesting that his prophecy includes more promises of the Messiah than any other book except Isaiah. One portion of the book is especially rich with such promises. It is that part in which the phrase 'in that day' occurs like a steady drumbeat (12:1–14:20).

Old Testament prophets used the phrase 'the day of the LORD' to refer to any dramatic intervention of God in human history, but Zechariah used it in a sharper and narrower way, namely, as a reference to the entire gospel age, which began with the first coming of Christ and which will close at the end of time.

The paramount feature of this gospel age is presented in the words of our text. It will be the age of a fountain opened for cleansing.

The cleansing fountain needed (v. 1)

Zechariah does not leave us in suspense about the nature of the cleansing that he has in mind. It is cleansing 'for sin and for uncleanness'.

Sin is the worst kind of filth there is. How few are serious about this serious thing!

What is sin? It is failing to conform to the laws of God. It is the creature thumbing his or her nose at the Creator and saying, 'I will not walk in your way! I will go my own way.'

It is refusing to do those things that God has explicitly commanded, choosing rather to do those things that God has plainly forbidden.

Why is sin so serious? Because it insults the God who has made us and blessed us, and this God is both holy and mighty. His holiness means that he must pronounce judgement upon sin, and his mightiness means that he has the power to bring upon us the judgement that he pronounces.

What is the judgement that the holy God has pronounced upon our sin? It is nothing less than eternal separation from himself and all that is good and glorious (2 Thes. 1:9).

Sin is defilement of the deepest dye. No soap can remove it. No launderer can expunge it. It requires special cleansing, and, wonder of wonders, the very God who is so profoundly offended by our sin has provided cleansing for it.

The cleansing fountain provided (v. 1)

What is the nature of this cleansing that God has provided for sin? Zechariah pictures it as an open fountain.

The word 'fountain' suggests a plenteous and continuous supply. The fact that it is open suggests availability.

What is this fountain? It is the Lord Jesus Christ shedding his blood on the cross of Calvary, as William Cowper affirms in words that are both well known and ever new:

> There is a fountain filled with blood
> Drawn from Immanuel's veins;
> And sinners plunged beneath that flood,
> Lose all their guilty stains.

It is true, of course, that Zechariah does not mention blood, but he does mention cleansing from sin. And the testimony of Scripture is that Jesus' blood cleanses from sin (Col. 1:14; 1 John 1:7).

It seems to be indescribably ridiculous and absurd to suggest that the blood Jesus shed on the cross actually cleanses from sin. What is there about his blood that makes it effective in the cleansing of sin? It has nothing to do with the chemical make-up of the blood itself. Jesus' blood has cleansing power because it was poured out on the cross, and blood poured out means life has been laid down. D. Martyn Lloyd-Jones says, '... the "blood" in Scripture means "life laid down in death." ... The blood is the final proof of the fact that death has been accomplished. It is not life preserved, it is life given up, it is life which has been laid down.'[1]

The penalty God has pronounced upon sin is eternal death (Rom. 6:23). That penalty is the expression of God's holy justice. God himself cannot set it aside without compromising his holy character. That penalty has to be paid either by the sinner personally or by someone in his or her stead.

The Lord Jesus came to pay that penalty on behalf of his people. He had no sins of his own, so he was able to pay for the sins of others. The cross was the place where he made that payment. There he endured the wrath of God in the place of sinners. The blood poured from him there, and he died. But his death was more than physical in nature. His physical sufferings and death were certainly horrific beyond description, but the sharpest part of his suffering lay in being abandoned by his Father so that those who believe in him will never have to be so abandoned. He went to hell on that cross so that his people will never have to go there themselves. His shed blood meant that his life had been poured out in this special kind of death. It meant that the greatest life that had ever been lived had ended in the greatest death ever died. It signalled the fact that he had accomplished his mission and had completely satisfied the justice of God.

Sinners laden with the burden and guilt of their sin can see in that cross a fountain of blood. They can see in the blood that Jesus shed sufficient payment for their own sins, and, trusting in the same, can find the relief and joy of forgiveness.

We must take note of the truth that this fountain of blood is made available to all. Zechariah says it is opened 'for the house of David and for the inhabitants of Jerusalem' (v. 1).

The house of David refers to the leadership of the nation, and the fountain would certainly be opened for them. But the same fountain would also be opened for the common citizens. It would not be a fountain only for the rich, educated and powerful. No one is too good for the cleansing blood of Christ, and, thank God, no one is too bad. That fountain can cleanse the worst of sinners! Matthew Henry notes that the fountain suggests 'inexhaustible fulness'. He proceeds to write, 'There is mercy enough in God, and merit enough in Christ, for the forgiving of the greatest sins and sinners, upon gospel-terms.'[2]

William Cowper writes,

> The dying thief rejoiced to see
> That fountain in his day;
> And there may I, though vile as he,
> Wash all my sins away.

What about Zechariah and his contemporaries, who were living centuries before the Lord Jesus was born in Bethlehem? If the fountain was opened when Jesus died on the cross, how were the people of the Old Testament forgiven of their sins? Did God have a different plan of salvation for them?

The Bible calls Jesus 'the Lamb slain from the foundation of the world' (Rev. 13:8). God has had only one plan of salvation, and that plan consists of his Son shedding his blood on the cross. Throughout the Old Testament era, God gave promises and pictures of his Son's coming death, and people of that era were forgiven as they looked forwards in faith to the fulfilment of God's promises. All the saved are saved through faith in the Lord Jesus. The only difference is that those who lived before Christ were saved as they looked forwards in faith to what he would do, while those of us on this side of the cross are saved as we look backwards in faith to what Christ has done. But it always Christ, and all of Christ.

The cleansing fountain cleansing (v. 2)

The prophet Zechariah calls our attention to yet another matter of vital importance. The fountain of blood that God opened for cleansing actually cleanses.

In this verse Zechariah mentions cleansing from idolatry and false teaching. He chose these sins because they were the major evils of the day. These sins were hand in glove. Spiralling idolatry was due in large measure to false prophets promoting false gods. Cleansing from these things would signal true and thorough cleansing indeed.

Zechariah's words are urgently needed in these days when so many are suggesting that we can be truly saved and yet go right on living as we did before. Some even go so far as to suggest that it is possible to be a 'carnal Christian', that is, one who is saved but goes on living in sin. It is, of course, possible for a Christian to act carnally from time to time, but that is a far cry from acting carnally all the time. Falling into a puddle of mud is not the same as living in it.

The teaching of the New Testament is that salvation makes us different (2 Cor. 5:17). It breaks the power and dominion of sin in our lives. The sins that remain are something like guerrilla soldiers who continue to fight for their cause after their army has been defeated and the peace treaty has been signed. The grace that defeats the army of sin will continue to help us against these guerrilla soldiers, and it will ultimately take us to heaven, where our battle against sin will finally end. Cowper's hymn gloriously declares,

> Dear dying Lamb, Thy precious blood
> Shall never lose its power
> Till all the ransomed church of God
> Be saved, to sin no more.

Michael Bentley summarizes the matter:

> Changes have to be made when people are cleansed from their sin and impurity. God declares, 'Once you have been justified (made righteous), you need to be sanctified (the process of being made holy).' This is a lifelong procedure. God's people are required to live holy lives and they should strive after a life given over entirely to God and obedience to his commands.'[3]

We cannot take our leave of this ancient prophecy from Zechariah without thinking again of how very blessed we are to have this fountain. Forgiveness of our sins and eternal glory belong to each believer in Christ because of the fountain of blood God opened on Calvary. May God help us to glory in that fountain, joining Cowper in singing,

E'er since, by faith, I saw the stream
Thy flowing wounds supply,
Redeeming love has been my theme,
And shall be till I die.

Reflect on these points

1. *Sin is defilement of the deepest dye. It requires special cleansing, and, wonder of wonders, the very God who is so profoundly offended by our sin has provided cleansing for it.*

2. *Jesus went to hell on that cross so that his people will never have to go there themselves. His shed blood meant that his life had been poured out. It signalled the fact that he had accomplished his mission and had completely satisfied the justice of God.*

3. *Salvation makes us different. The sins that remain are like guerrilla soldiers who continue to fight for their cause after their army has been defeated and the peace treaty has been signed. The grace that defeats the army of sin will continue to help us against these guerrilla soldiers, and it will ultimately take us to heaven, where our battle against sin will finally end.*

The Prophet
Malachi

Our listening God[1]

'Your words have been harsh against Me,' says the LORD, 'yet you say, "What have we spoken against You?"

You have said, "It is useless to serve God; what profit is it that we have kept His ordinance, and that we have walked as mourners before the LORD of hosts?

So now we call the proud blessed, for those who do wickedness are raised up; they even tempt God and go free."'

Then those who feared the LORD spoke to one another, and the LORD listened and heard them; so a book of remembrance was written before Him for those who fear the LORD and who meditate on His name.

'They shall be Mine,' says the LORD of hosts, 'on the day that I make them My jewels. And I will spare them as a man spares his own son who serves him.'

Then you shall again discern between the righteous and the wicked, between one who serves God and one who does not serve Him.

Malachi 3:13–18

Malachi ('my messenger') is the last of the post-exilic prophets. That means he ministered after the exile, or captivity. The captivity refers, of course, to the period the Jewish people spent in Babylon.

After the decree that freed them from Babylon, the Jews began returning to their land. Zerubbabel led the first group of captives, consisting of 50,000, in 536 BC (Ezra 1:5–2:70; Neh. 12).

One of the major accomplishments of this group of returnees

was rebuilding the temple and restoring the sacrificial system (516 BC).

In 458 BC, Ezra led a second group. In 445 BC, Nehemiah led yet another group. Nehemiah was appointed governor of the Jewish nation by King Artaxerxes of Persia.

Things progressed rapidly under Nehemiah. The walls of Jerusalem were rebuilt, and a spiritual renewal took place.

But Nehemiah was called back to Persia on business and was absent from Jerusalem from 432 to 425 BC (Neh. 2:6; 5:14; 13:6).

It was during the years of his absence that Malachi conducted his prophetic ministry.

As noted above, the temple had been rebuilt and the sacrifices had resumed before Malachi came onto the scene. The walls of Jerusalem had also been constructed. Many good things had been achieved in the long, tortuous task of rebuilding the nation.

But while good things had happened, Malachi's was not a good time. Miles Bennett describes the situation in this way: 'A spirit of dull depression had settled over the inhabitants of Jerusalem; skepticism and spiritual indifference held the people in their grasp ... The flood of skepticism abroad in the land affected both the people and their religious leaders. Religion became largely a matter of ritual. Apathy and stinginess towards God prevailed.'[2]

How did the people get into such a state? Joyce Baldwin answers: '... the Temple had been completed, but nothing momentous had occurred to indicate that God's presence had returned to fill it with glory ...'[3]

In other words, nothing had happened to indicate that the glorious prophecies of Haggai and Zechariah were going to be fulfilled. Consequently, in the words of Baldwin, 'The round of religious duties continued to be carried on, but without enthusiasm.'[4]

Is this prophecy really of critical importance for us? Is it worthy of our time and attention? We must say that we can ignore it only if we are not:

- sputtering in our faith
- offering half-hearted devotion to the Lord
- ignoring the commandments of the Lord.

Our own hearts will tell us whether these things are true of us. If they are, we need the good medicine of Malachi.

God's answer to the condition of the people was to send Malachi to carry on a dialogue with the people. There are seven occurrences of dialogue in which God makes an accusation, the people raise an objection and God refutes the objection (1:2–5; 1:6–2:9; 2:10–14; 2:15–17; 3:6–7; 3:8–12; 3:13–15).

The verses of our text focus our attention on God's awareness of everything people say. Such knowledge, along with the realization that words will be judged by God (Matt. 12:36–37), should make us very careful!

God listening to words of complaint (vv. 13–15)

THE LORD CONFRONTS THEM (V. 13)

The Lord charges the people of Israel with speaking harshly against him, and, just as they did with each of his previous charges, the people dispute the charge by asking, 'What have we spoken against You?' That amounted to them saying, 'We have done no such thing!' They did not seem to realize that their quarrelling with God proved his point!

THE LORD QUOTES THEM (VV. 14–15)

God proceeds to show them how they had spoken against him. No, they had not said 'God is bad' or 'God is mean.' But they had said 'It is useless to serve God' (v. 14).

As the Lord continues to quote their own words back to them, we cannot help but conclude that they are taking too much credit. They claim that they have 'kept His ordinance', that is, obeyed his commands. They also profess to have 'walked as mourners' before the Lord. As John Benton points out, mourners at a funeral are 'careful to be on their best behaviour'.[5]

The people are claiming to have been very well behaved and very careful about serving the Lord!

After all this faithful, careful serving they have supposedly done, they draw the monstrous conclusion that it is better to be wicked than to be righteous (v. 15)! The proud are more blessed than the humble! The wicked are built up while the righteous are torn down! Those who thumb their noses at God get away with it!

Others in the Bible came to this same melancholy conclusion. Asaph, the author of Psalm 73, writes,

> But as for me, my feet had almost stumbled;
>
> My steps had nearly slipped.
>
> For I was envious of the boastful,
>
> When I saw the prosperity of the wicked.
>
> (vv. 2–3)

A bit later he adds,

> Behold, these are the ungodly,
>
> Who are always at ease;
>
> They increase in riches.
>
> Surely I have cleansed my heart in vain.
>
> And washed my hands in innocence.
>
> For all day long I have been plagued,
>
> And chastened every morning.
>
> (vv. 12–14)

Many believers today have no trouble identifying with Asaph!

We cannot come away from this section without asking ourselves whether we are as guilty as Malachi's people. Do we claim too much for ourselves in terms of serving the Lord? Do we suggest, by the way that we go about the Lord's work, that it is a very dreary and meaningless affair? Do we find ourselves envying those who are not 'burdened' with serving the Lord? Do we yearn to be free from serving the Lord? If we speak against serving God, we have spoken against God!

God listening to words of encouragement (vv. 16–18)

WHO SPOKE THESE WORDS?

Malachi describes them as 'those who fear the LORD' and 'meditate on His name' (v. 16). What does it mean to fear God? It is to stand in awe of his person, to submit to his authority and to dread his displeasure. Christians are not casual or nonchalant about God!

We should note that Malachi simply states this as a fact. He doesn't say that the righteous should fear the Lord, but he matter-of-factly observes that they do.

If this is true of the righteous, it's simple logic to conclude that the unrighteous do not fear the Lord. The Bible flatly asserts this: 'There is no fear of God before their eyes' (Rom. 3:18).

The ungodly refuse to be afraid of God when there is reason to be afraid.

TO WHOM DID THEY SPEAK, AND WHAT DID THEY SAY?

These people spoke to 'one another'. Those who feared the Lord spoke to others who feared the Lord. John Benton writes, 'Some people realized that if they went on much longer in this climate of conversation, where all they heard poured scorn on God, then very soon they too would end up bitter and faithless. Their response was to seek each other out and to talk together.'[6]

While the text does not specify what these people said, the fact that they all feared the Lord means that they spoke words consistent with that fear and words that would encourage and promote it.

The Lord promised to remember them (v. 16)
The Jews were familiar with the idea of kings recording the names of those who had done good (Esth. 6:1–2). God also has such a book. It consists of the names of the God-fearers of whom he has been speaking. We are not to conclude from this that God has a bad memory. It is rather God stooping to their level to speak in a way they could easily understand. He was assuring them that he would not forget those who did not forget him! The God with perfect memory keeps perfect records!

The Lord promised a special privilege (v. 17)
The Lord would not only remember these people but he would also treat them as his own special treasure on that glorious day when he makes up his jewels. The thought is that God's people are jewels who are scattered and mired in the mud of this world. But, at the end, he will find them all, put them into his treasure chest and will look upon them with pride and satisfaction. They will be his crown jewels. God's people may not appear to be much now, but they will be known to be much then (see Dan. 12:3).

The Lord promised a clear distinction (v. 18)
The difference between believers and unbelievers may not always be apparent in this life, but, in the words of T. V.

111

Moore, there is coming a '… great day of final adjustment … in which all seeming anomalies of the present shall be fully explained and wholly removed forever.'[7]

What day is this great day? It is the day when this life is over and eternity finally dawns.

On that day, the debate about whether or not it is wise to serve God will for ever cease. To the people of Malachi's day, it often appeared that there was no point in being righteous. The line between the righteous and the wicked was so horribly blurred that it seemed as if one was as good as another. But eternity will bring clarity to all muddled situations, and it will be obvious then that the righteous were wise. Like the people of Malachi's generation, we sometimes envy the wicked, but no one will envy them in eternity.

We may not be able to detect much difference between the righteous and the wicked here. They may appear to be equally blessed and, in some instances, the wicked may appear to be even more blessed. But when the eternal day dawns, the difference will be plain for all to see.

The people of God are not to expect him to vindicate them finally in this life. We get into deep trouble when we expect this life to yield the things that only eternity can yield.

We are further called not to envy the wicked but to feel deep compassion and pity for them. The happiness they enjoy in this life is all the happiness they will know. Asaph was at first troubled by the prosperity of the wicked, but he came to see that it is utter foolishness to envy anyone who is headed for eternal destruction (Ps. 73:17–20).

Reflect on these points

1. Are we as guilty as Malachi's people? Do we claim too much for ourselves in terms of serving the Lord? Do we suggest, by the way that we go about the Lord's work, that it is dreary and meaningless? Do we envy those who are not 'burdened' with serving the Lord? If we speak against serving God, we have spoken against God!

2. What does it mean to fear God? It is to stand in awe of his person, submit to his authority and dread his displeasure. Christians are not casual or nonchalant about God!

3. God was assuring them that he would not forget those who did not forget him! The God with perfect memory keeps perfect records! God will find them all, put them into his treasure chest and will look upon them with pride and satisfaction. They will be his crown jewels. God's people may not appear to be much now, but they will be known to be much then.

4. The people of God are not to expect him to vindicate them finally in this life. We get into deep trouble when we expect this life to yield the things that only eternity can yield.

5. We are called not to envy the wicked but to feel deep compassion and pity for them. The happiness they enjoy in this life is all the happiness they will know.

Endnotes

Joel

1   John Calvin, *Commentaries*, vol. xiv (Grand Rapids, MI: Baker Book House, 1979), p. 58.

2   Duane A. Garrett, *The New American Commentary*, vol. xiv (a) (Nashville, TN: Broadman & Holman), p. 348.

Amos

1   Matthew Henry, *Matthew Henry's Commentary*, vol. iv ((n.p.) Fleming H. Revell (n.d.)), p. 1268.

Obadiah

1   *New Geneva Study Bible* (Nashville, TN: Thomas Nelson, 1995), p. 1412.

Jonah

1   O. Palmer Robertson, *Jonah: A Study in Compassion* (Edinburgh: Banner of Truth, 1990), p. 13.

2   Ibid., p. 16.

3   Ibid., p. 60.

Micah

1   John Gill, *Exposition of the Old and New Testaments*, vol. vi (Paris, AR: The Baptist Standard Bearer, 1989), p. 593.

2   Kenneth L. Barker, *New American Commentary*, vol. xx, p. 135.

3   Ibid., p. 135.

4   Charles Spurgeon, *Metropolitan Tabernacle Pulpit*, vol. lviii (Pasadena, TX: Pilgrim Publications, 1979), pp. 409–410.

Nahum

1   Waylon Bailey, *New American Commentary*, vol. xx, p. 178.

2   J. N. Heflin, *Nahum, Habakkuk, Zephaniah, and Haggai* (Bible Study Commentary; Grand Rapids, MI: Zondervan, 1985), p. 44.

Habakkuk

1 Bailey, *New American Commentary*, vol. xx, p. 375.
2 Ibid.
3 Ibid., p. 377.

Zephaniah

1 A similar chapter appears in my book *The Guide to Christian Comfort* (Darlington: Evangelical Press, 2003), pp. 118–125).
2 Alexander Maclaren, *Expositions of Holy Scripture*, vol. vi (Grand Rapids, MI; Baker Book House, 1974), p. 248.

Zechariah

1 D. Martyn Lloyd-Jones, *Romans: An Exposition of Chapters 3.20–4.25* (Grand Rapids, MI: Zondervan, 1970), p. 87.
2 Henry, *Commentary*, p. 1464.
3 Michael Bentley, *Building for God's Glory* (Darlington: Evangelical Press, 1989), p. 209.

Malachi

1 A similar chapter appears in my book *Opening up Malachi* (Leominster: Day One, 2007), pp. 58–62.
2 T. Miles Bennett, *The Broadman Bible Commentary*, vol. vii (Nashville, TN: Broadman Press, 1972), p. 368.
3 Joyce G. Baldwin, *Haggai, Zechariah, Malachi* (Tyndale Old Testament Commentaries; Leicester: Inter-Varsity Press), p. 211.
4 Ibid.
5 John Benton, *Losing Touch with the Living God* (Welwyn: Evangelical Press, 1985), p. 112.
6 Ibid., p. 117.
7 T.V. Moore, *Zechariah, Haggai and Malachi* (Edinburgh: Banner of Truth, 1974), pp. 167–8.

About Day One:

Day One's threefold commitment:
- To be faithful to the Bible, God's inerrant, infallible Word;
- To be relevant to our modern generation;
- To be excellent in our publication standards.

I continue to be thankful for the publications of Day One. They are biblical; they have sound theology; and they are relevant to the issues at hand. The material is condensed and manageable while, at the same time, being complete—a challenging balance to find. We are happy in our ministry to make use of these excellent publications.

JOHN MACARTHUR, PASTOR-TEACHER, GRACE COMMUNITY CHURCH, CALIFORNIA

It is a great encouragement to see Day One making such excellent progress. Their publications are always biblical, accessible and attractively produced, with no compromise on quality. Long may their progress continue and increase!

JOHN BLANCHARD, AUTHOR, EVANGELIST AND APOLOGIST

Visit our web site for more information and
to request a free catalogue of our books.

www.dayone.co.uk

When Heaven calls your name

People in the Bible who heard God speak

ROGER ELLSWORTH

128PP, PAPERBACK

ISBN 978-1-84625-102-3

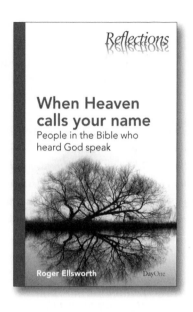

Believing that repetition indicates emphasis, Roger Ellsworth examines occasions in the Bible in which God the Father or God the Son repeated someone's name. He asserts that these instances were meant to make certain truths 'dance' before our eyes. In an increasingly difficult and challenging world, these truths will thrill, comfort and guide all those who genuinely embrace them.

'God speaks. He has spoken, and he continues to speak today. Through these vivid portraits of Heaven's calls, you will overhear the voice of God speaking specifically and clearly to you.'
TODD BRADY, PASTOR OF THE FIRST BAPTIST CHURCH OF PADUCAH, KENTUCKY, USA

Roger Ellsworth has given us another book full of pastoral integrity and fidelity to the Word of God. *When Heaven calls your name* is both exegetically sound and devotionally warm—a book that is as heart-stirring as it is instructional. The readers of this book who hear their names called will grow in the faith and knowledge of our Lord and Saviour, Jesus Christ. I heartily recommend it!
IVAN SCHOEN, PASTOR, MARANATHA BAPTIST CHURCH, POPLAR GROVE, ILLINOIS, USA

Under God's smile

The Trinitarian Blessing of
2 Corinthians 13:14

DEREK PRIME

128PP, PAPERBACK

ISBN 978-1-84625-059-0

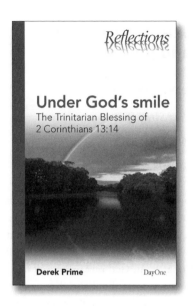

During recent decades, it has become the practice of Christians in many churches and in university and college Christian Unions to commit one another to God's grace and care with the words 'May the grace of the Lord Jesus Christ, and the love of God, and the fellowship of the Holy Spirit be with us all' (2 Corinthians 13:14). They are familiar words, but what do they actually mean? For what are we praying?

So that we do not repeat these words without appreciating their full implication, Derek Prime explores them and considers the three Persons of the Trinity in their different, yet perfectly harmonious, relationship to every believer. Written in an easy-to-read style, this book is thoroughly rooted in the Scriptures and is a demonstration that solid biblical truth is both heart-warming and exciting.

'Wholesome food for the average Christian reader and devotional writing of the highest order'
EVANGELICALS NOW

'An easily-read book, helpful in all stages of Christian life'
GRACE MAGAZINE

'Derek Prime's ministry is much appreciated by many Christian groups, including ourselves. Like all his other books ... biblically based and easy to read'
ASSOCIATED PRESBYTERIANS NEWS

'If, like me, you are constantly on the lookout for books that say a great deal in short order, you will be delighted by what you hold in your hand. It is a special gift not only to expound what the blessing of the triune God means, but also to explain why it matters. We have come to expect this from Derek Prime, and once again he hits the mark.'
ALISTAIR BEGG, SENIOR PASTOR, PARKSIDE CHURCH, CHAGRIN FALLS, OHIO

Seasons of comfort and joy

Meditations in verse based on select Scritpture readings

ANNE STANDFIELD

96PP, PAPERBACK

ISBN 978-1-84625-103-0

God's Word, the Bible, is the guidebook to life for all people. It is the 'measuring rod' or standard by which we live out our lives before God, the Creator of all things. In it, God reveals himself to us and teaches us about ourselves and the world around us. God's Word is vital in revealing the truth to each of us; only the Bible teaches us how sinful people can ever be reconciled to a holy God.

In these warm, Christ-centred poems, Anne Standfield demonstrates her joy in the truths of God's Word, sharing her experiences of God and the knowledge of his Word with others with a view that they, with her, 'may know him better' (Ephesians 1:17). All the poems have been based solely upon Scripture with the aim that each reader may come to know the only true God and Jesus Christ, his Son, whom he has sent as our Saviour. This is the only way to eternal life (John 17:3).

Reflections

Seasons of comfort and joy
Meditations in verse based on select Scripture readings

Anne Standfield   DayOne

Read some sample poems on the following pages

Carried

[Based on Isaiah 46:3–5.]

O God of all strength,
　　Who is like unto you?
He who bears us from birth
　　And will carry us through;
He who shines in our darkness,
　　Brings us hope in despair,
In whose arms we are resting;
　　Who with you can compare?

Isaiah 46:4:
'… I have made you and I will carry you; I will sustain you and I will rescue you.'

Eternal mystery

[Based on Ephesians 1:7–14.]

Oh, the riches of God's grace,
　　Lavished all on me,
In making known his wondrous plan—
　　His eternal mystery!
For in the purpose of his will
　　He chose me in his Son;
My heart now sings his glorious praise
　　For all that he has done!

Ephesians 1:11–12:
'In him we were also chosen, having been predestined according to the plan of him who works out everything in conformity with the purpose of his will, in order that we, who were the first to hope in Christ, might be for the praise of his glory.'

Daystar

[Based on Revelation 22:16.]

Revelation 22:16:
'I, Jesus ... am the Root and the Offspring of David, and the bright Morning Star.'

The lengthening of days and the
    shortening of nights,
    Reversal of yonder celestial lights,
The day has arisen to show unto all
    Dominion of light over darkest nightfall.
God's Daystar arises within every heart
    To shine on forever, and ne'er to depart;
Sin's darkness he cleanses and evil dispels
    In every believer whose heart he indwells.

Eternal Lamb

[Based on Isaiah 53:6.]

Isaiah 53:6:
'We all, like sheep, have gone astray, each of us has turned to his own way; and the Lord has laid on him the iniquity of us all.'

The eternal Lamb of God
    Has shed his precious blood
To bring the wanderers to the fold
    And lead us back to God.
So raise salvation's song
    To realms beyond the sky;
For God's own Son has sacrificed
    His life, that sin may die!

Unless

[Based on Matthew 7:18, 20.]

Matthew 7:18, 20:
'A good tree cannot bear bad fruit, and a bad tree cannot bear good fruit …
Thus, by their fruit you will recognize them.'

Unless we show how much we care
     To each and every one,
How can one know Christ's love is there
Within our hearts, unless we share
          God's only Son?

Unless the love of Christ abides,
          And we his fruit can see,
How can we know that one has cried
Unto the Lord, the crucified,
          And been made free?

Unless we love as Christ has loved,
          How can one simply know
That Christ indwells us from above?
That we are filled with heavenly love?
          Unless we show?

Unless that love of Christ is shown,
          How does one know there's care?
How does one know love's been made known
To those who say Christ's Name they own
          Unless they share?

Steal not tomorrow

[Based on Psalm 31:14–15.]

Psalm 31:14–15:
'But I trust in you, O Lord; I say, "You are my God." My times are in your hands …'

Steal not tomorrow out of the Father's hand,
  For the time has not yet come to fulfil what he has planned;
Those moments are as precious as the many hours that pass,
    But rest assured that, in his time, the answer comes at last.

God answers every prayer that a repentant sinner prays,
    Yet it may not be the answer of our own desired way;
Sometimes it comes as 'No', and very often, 'Wait',
    But no prayer goes unanswered that a true believer makes.

The precious school of patience he has called you to attend
    To teach you there the meaning of an even better end.
He has not left you to endure without a cause in sight,
    He knows that, by your waiting, you will learn his way is right.

And when that time has come when tomorrow is today,
    And the answer's been revealed in the most diverse of ways,
Just thank the precious Father that he's ended all your sorrow
    And spare a thought for someone who is praying for tomorrow.

Incarnation

[Based on Micah 5:2–5.]

Of origin of old,
   Sent forth from ancient times,
The Ruler from on high—
Eternally sublime!
     His government shall know no end,
     The King of kings, the sinner's Friend.

Great Shepherd of the sheep,
In majesty arrayed,
Came forth to realms of time,
Was in a manger laid.
     Our peace he is, we live secure;
     His greatness reigns for evermore.

The Holy One of God—
Incarnate Deity—
Was born of virgin's womb
In meek humility!
     O mighty Ruler, come and reign
     Within those hearts that love your Name.

Micah 5:2:
'But you,
Bethlehem
Ephrathah,
though you are
small among the
clans of Judah,
out of you will
come for me
one who will be
ruler over Israel,
whose origins are
from of old, from
ancient times.'

Reflections

They echoed the voice of God

Reflections on the Minor Prophets

Many carry a little Bible and believe in a little God. Their Bibles are little because they ignore so many of its books. Their God is little because they ignore so many of the Bible's truths. The Minor Prophets can help us. These men made sense of their circumstances and found strength for their challenges by basking in the presence of the God who was above it all and in it all. The God they served was wise enough to plan, and strong enough to achieve. This study of their messages will help us have both bigger Bibles and a bigger God.

'Roger Ellsworth helps us appreciate how the so-called Minor Prophets make known the character and work of our great God. This book is a great introduction to and overview of their prophecies.'

Tom Ascol, Director of Founders Minist *and Pastor, Grace Baptist Church, Cap* *Coral, Florida*

'In this excellent book on the Minor Prophets, Roger Ellsworth gives the reader a clear understanding of the importance of these neglected and oft underestimated books of the Bible. Ro Ellsworth goes on to show clearly how of these men demonstrated the greatn of God in their message—a message a essential for our day as it was for their *Jim Winter, Minister of Horsell Evangel. Church, Woking, England*

Roger Ellswort is the pastor of Covenant of Grac Baptist Church, Salem, Illinois. He the author of over thirty books, including several titles published by Day One. He and his wife, Sylvia, have two sons and two grandchildren.

Day One Publications
Ryelands Road Leominster HR6 8NZ
Email: sales@dayone.co.uk | www.dayone.co.uk
☎ +44 (0) 1568 613 740 | FAX 01568 611 473
☎ Toll Free 888 329 6630 (North America)

DayOne

ISBN: 978-1846251016

9 781846 251016 >

£!